Cicerone
County Walking Series

WALKING IN WARWICKSHIRE

*William Shakespeare is buried in Holy Trinity Church
on the banks of his beloved Avon at Stratford*

WALKING IN WARWICKSHIRE

by
Brian Conduit

CICERONE PRESS
MILNTHORPE, CUMBRIA

© Brian Conduit 1998
ISBN 1 85284 255 5
A catalogue record for this book is available from the British Library.

Acknowledgements

I am greatly indebted to Stuart Ikeringill, Countryside Access Officer of Warwickshire County Council, for the invaluable advice and assistance that he has given me throughout the preparation of this book.

OTHER BOOKS IN THIS SERIES

Walking in Cornwall
Walking in Cheshire
Walking in Dorset
Walking in Devon
Walking in Durham

Walking in the Isle of Wight
Walking in Kent (2 vols)
Walking in Lancashire
Walking in Oxfordshire

FORTHCOMING

Walking in Northumberland
Walking in Sussex

Walking in Somerset

CICERONE BOOKS BY THE SAME AUTHOR

Heritage Trails in NW England

Front Cover: Kenilworth Castle

CONTENTS

Advice to Readers

Readers are advised that whilst every effort is taken by the author to ensure the accuracy of this guidebook, changes can occur which may affect the contents. It is advisable to check locally on transport, accommodation, shops etc but even rights-of-way can be altered.

The publisher would welcome notes of any such changes

LOCATION OF
THE WALKS

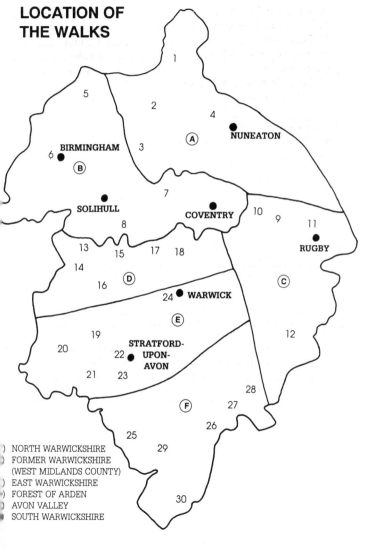

1

5

2

4

● NUNEATON

Ⓐ

3

6 ● BIRMINGHAM

Ⓑ

7

● SOLIHULL

● COVENTRY

10

9

11

● RUGBY

8

13

15

17

18

14

16

Ⓓ

24 ● WARWICK

Ⓔ

19

STRATFORD-
UPON-
AVON

22 ●

12

20

21

23

28

27

Ⓕ

26

25

29

30

Ⓐ NORTH WARWICKSHIRE
Ⓑ FORMER WARWICKSHIRE
(WEST MIDLANDS COUNTY)
Ⓒ EAST WARWICKSHIRE
Ⓓ FOREST OF ARDEN
Ⓔ AVON VALLEY
Ⓕ SOUTH WARWICKSHIRE

*The splendid woodland of New Fallings Coppice
adjoins Earlswood Lakes
Walk 13*

INTRODUCTION

Warwickshire is my native county. At least I believe it is. I was born in Birmingham and at the time that city was geographically in Warwickshire. Indeed I lived only about a 20 minute walk from the Warwickshire County Cricket Ground at Edgbaston. Local government reorganisation in the 1970s moved my birthplace into the newly-created county of West Midlands but I still regard myself as a son of Warwickshire.

That item of personal information partly explains why the Warwickshire that is covered by this walking guide is the traditional county, the one that has existed for centuries, not the truncated one that was left after the changes of the 1970s. It therefore includes those parts of the West Midlands - the boroughs of Birmingham, Coventry and Solihull - that were previously in Warwickshire.

'Mid-most England'

The American writer Henry James described Warwickshire as 'mid-most England' and it is true that in almost every conceivable way - geography, size and landscape - the county is the very essence of Middle England. Geographically it lies at the heart of the country; a cross on the village green at Meriden, roughly half way between Birmingham and Coventry, is reputed to mark the exact centre of England. Its size places it in the middle ranks of English counties, and its pleasant, gently rolling landscapes must be what every exiled Englishman dreams of when feeling nostalgic for his homeland.

Many Warwickshire villages can compete with any in those parts of the country, like Devon and the Cotswolds, that are perhaps better known for the quality and attractiveness of their villages. The county possesses some very pleasant small towns, such as Henley-in-Arden, Shipston-on-Stour, Coleshill and Alcester, and two outstanding historic towns in Stratford-upon-Avon and Warwick. There are no medieval cathedrals or major monastic remains but Warwickshire is renowned for its wealth of Tudor buildings and it does have two of the finest castles in the country at Warwick and Kenilworth, as well as some charming small manor houses and larger country mansions. It goes almost without saying that within its traditional boundaries it embraces two major cities, including Britain's second city.

On every main road leading into Warwickshire, the signs proudly proclaim that you are entering 'Shakespeare's County' and the most visited area, and one of the most attractive areas, is that around Stratford-upon-Avon. The bard is undoubtedly the county's most famous son and does more for the local tourist industry than anyone else, but there is a lot more to Warwickshire than the Elizabethan buildings and Shakespearean sites around Stratford, so beloved by native and foreign visitors alike, delightful and fascinating though these may be.

Arden and Feldon

Threading its way through Shakespeare Country and the heart of Warwickshire is the lovely River Avon, the boundary between Arden and Feldon, the two halves into which the county was traditionally divided. Arden, the woodland, was the area to the north of the river, a relatively poor agricultural region of sandy soils, heathland and forest. The Feldon, the field land, lay to the south, a more open, intensively farmed and prosperous region of arable fields and sheep pastures. The 16th century traveller Leland points out the contrasts between them. Arden is described as 'not so plentifull of corne, but of grasse and woode' whereas Feldon is 'baren of woode but plentifull of corne'.

Both parts have their quota of attractive villages, but in Arden they are mainly of brick and timber and the churches are relatively small. In the Feldon the villages are predominantly stone-built and, as a result of the greater prosperity, the churches tend to be larger and more ornate. Some of them were built from the profits of the local wool trade and rank with the great 'wool churches' of the Cotswolds further south. The main hills in the south of the county - Brailes, Burton Dassett, Edge Hill, Ilmington Downs - are part of the Jurassic limestone range that includes the Cotswolds and continues across this corner of Warwickshire into Northamptonshire and beyond. Feldon is mainly limestone country, Arden is predominantly sandstone country; the Avon therefore is also a geological boundary.

Industrial Revolution

A major change to the landscape of parts of Warwickshire came during the Industrial Revolution. Coal mining had been carried out in the north-east of the county since as early as the 14th century but the industry grew rapidly in the Victorian era. At the same time the north-west became heavily urbanised with the expansion of the medieval city of Coventry and the massive growth of Birmingham. The latter hungrily devoured much of the surrounding area, gathering former rural villages into its suburbs.

Industrial growth created the need for transport improvements and a network of canals was built across the county to link the manufactures of Birmingham and Coventry with their markets. The towpaths of these canals now make excellent walking routes. Canals were followed by railways, roads and finally motorways and Warwickshire has its fair share of the latter. Industries are a temporary phenomenon and most of the coal mines have now disappeared and their sites, and some other areas of industrial spoilation in the north, have become green again and been successfully reclaimed for agriculture, nature or recreation.

Walking in Warwickshire

The most frequent adjectives that writers seem to use when describing the scenery of Warwickshire are 'pleasant' and 'undramatic'. True, there are no majestic and rugged landscapes, as in the Lake District or Snowdonia, no wild and lonely expanses of moorland, as in the Pennines or Dartmoor, not even areas of open downland, as in Dorset, Wiltshire or Sussex. The highest point in the county on Ilmington Down rises to around 850 feet, lower than the hills of neighbouring Worcestershire. What the walker in Warwickshire will find is a gentle landscape of well-wooded slopes, undulating pastures and arable fields, rich parklands and slowly meandering rivers. Dotted around it are old farmhouses and medieval manor houses, small market towns and attractive villages of brick and stone, with thatched and timber-framed buildings, medieval churches and welcoming inns, a particularly appealing combination.

There are no challenging or difficult walks in this book. Given the nature of the terrain, it would be difficult to devise a really challenging walk except purely on the grounds of length. Everything is in moderation. Nobody walking in Warwickshire is likely to experience any of the difficulties or dangers that are always present in more rugged terrain with harsher climates. The main dangers are likely to be bulls or over zealous farm dogs; the main difficulty, as anywhere in Britain at certain times of the year, may well be mud.

Conditions are made easier by the high standards of waymarking and maintenance of the footpath network throughout the county, for which Warwickshire County Council is to be congratulated. Walkers are unlikely to encounter the familiar problems of broken-down stiles, absence of footbridges and blocked paths.

This makes the Warwickshire terrain ideal for family walking, from small children to grandparents. It is possible to walk safely at all seasons of the year and some of the walks will be particularly enjoyable on a firm, crisp, bright winter day when the views stand out clearly. You do not have to be an athletic superperson to try any of them. Some are lengthier and more strenuous than others, some will involve modest hill climbing; simply look at the distances and introductory details of each one and choose whichever is most suitable for you, taking into account your own capabilities, the time at your disposal and the current state of the weather.

Divisions

For the purposes of this walking guide, the county has been divided into six regions.

1. NORTH WARWICKSHIRE - lying to the north of the Birmingham-Coventry axis.

2. FORMER WARWICKSHIRE - those parts of the West Midlands county formerly in Warwickshire.

3. EAST WARWICKSHIRE - the area roughly to the east of the A423 Coventry-Banbury road.

4. FOREST OF ARDEN - between the West Midlands border and the Avon valley.

5. AVON VALLEY - the heart of the county and including the two main historic towns, Warwick and Stratford-upon-Avon.

6. SOUTH WARWICKSHIRE - the hilliest region of the county south of the Avon valley.

These divisions are somewhat arbitrary. For example, the old Forest of Arden extended over most of the north of the county, including many of the present suburbs of Birmingham, and Former Warwickshire is a purely administrative rather than a natural division. The purpose is simply to break the county down into manageable and convenient portions for the visitor who wants to appreciate the landscape, towns and villages, and historic sites of Warwickshire in the best possible way, that is by exploring its footpaths, bridleways and country lanes.

Accommodation
There is a wide range of accommodation to suit all preferences and incomes: cheap bed and breakfast in private homes, medium priced guesthouses and small hotels, self-catering establishments, farmhouses and luxury hotels. For details contact the local tourist information centres. (See Useful Organisations at the end of the book.)

Public Transport
Being in the centre of England, Warwickshire is not only the hub of the country's motorway and main road system, but is also the hub of the rail network and is well served by buses. A map and details of rail and bus services are available on a very useful leaflet produced by Warwickshire County Council and obtainable from tourist information centres. These details can also be obtained by telephoning the Warwickshire Traveline number: 01926 414140. For similar details for the West Midlands phone: 0121 200 2700.

COUNTRY CODE

Please observe this whenever you are walking in the countryside.

- Enjoy the countryside and respect its life and work
- Guard against all risk of fire
- Take your litter home
- Fasten all gates
- Help to keep all water clean
- Keep your dogs under control
- Protect wildlife, plants and trees
- Keep to public paths across farmland
- Take special care on country roads
- Leave livestock, crops and machinery alone
- Make no unnecessary noise
- Use gates and stiles to cross fences, hedges and walls

NORTH WARWICKSHIRE

Looking at a current map, this is the area of Warwickshire that has become almost detached from the main part of the county by the eastward bulge of the West Midlands, needed to incorporate Coventry. It lies basically to the north and north-east of the Birmingham-Coventry conurbation and tapers almost to a point at its northern extremity where it is bounded by Staffordshire and Leicestershire.

Apart from Birmingham and Coventry, this was the most industrialised part of the county, the area of the North Warwickshire coalfield based around Bedworth and Nuneaton. As this was never a large coalfield, it made a relatively minor impact on the landscape and even in its heyday, there was plenty of remaining open and unspoilt countryside. Now almost all the mines have gone and many of the industrial scars have disappeared due to successful landscaping and reclamation.

Two of the walks take you through areas reclaimed from former industrial eyesores. A third is based on a country park on the edge of Nuneaton, the largest town in North Warwickshire, and the fourth has a real feel of remoteness, despite distant glimpses of some of the tower blocks of Birmingham.

1. *Polesworth and Alvecote Priory*

Route:	Polesworth - Shuttington - Alvecote Priory - Coventry Canal - Polesworth
Start:	Polesworth, crossroads at bottom end of Bridge Street by bridge over River Anker
Distance:	6¹/₂ miles
Parking:	Polesworth
Refreshments:	Pubs and cafes at Polesworth, pub at Shuttington
OS Maps:	Landrangers 139 and 140
	Pathfinder 893

On such a pleasant walk, it is difficult to believe that this was once an area badly scarred by opencast mining. Now the main scar is the M42 motorway, crossed on the first leg of the route and passed under towards the end. The route first heads across fields to the hilltop village of Shuttington. From here there are fine views over the Anker valley and Alvecote Pools, the latter formed by mining subsidence and now a nature reserve. You then descend to the meagre ruins of Alvecote Priory, continue through the woodlands of the nature reserve and finally walk along the towpath of the Coventry Canal for an attractive return to Polesworth.

Start by taking the road signposted to Atherstone, turn left onto a tarmac path across grass, cross one bridge and keep ahead to cross another one over the River Anker. Continue across the riverside meadow and at a sign to 'Abbey Church', turn right along a path - later enclosed - to the church (A).

In front of the church, turn left along a track, passing a war memorial, and go under the Abbey Gateway to a road. Turn left, at a T-junction turn right, in the Shuttington direction, cross a railway bridge and keep ahead to a T-junction. Take the tarmac track opposite along the right edge of a field, pass through a gap in the field corner and the track curves right and passes to the left of a house. Climb a stile to the right of a brick building, walk across a field to climb another and continue along the left edge of a field to a track.

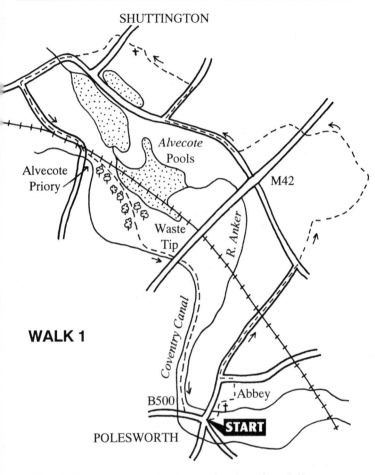

Turn left over a concrete bridge and head gently uphill, passing to the right of a farm and the derelict Bramcote Hall. Follow the track as it curves left, turns right to cross the M42 and then bends left to continue to a lane. Turn right, take the first turning on the right and look out for a waymarked stile on the left.

Climb it and keep along the right edge of a field, heading gently uphill and climbing three more stiles. After the third one, continue along a track for a few yards and turn right up steps to another stile. Climb that, walk along an enclosed path to emerge onto a track and immediately turn left to continue along an enclosed path into Shuttington churchyard. Walk through it, passing to the right of the church (B), go through a kissing gate and continue along a track to a road.

Keep ahead, passing in front of modern houses, follow the road to left and right and continue along a tarmac path to a stile. Climb it, and another a few yards ahead, to enter a field, bear left and head downhill, making for a double stile and a plank over a ditch. Cross these, continue in the same direction across the next field and climb a stile onto a road.

Keep ahead to cross Shuttington Bridge over the River Anker and take the first turning on the left, signposted to Alvecote and Wilnecote. Walk past the long terrace of Alvecote Cottages, turn right to cross first a railway bridge and then a canal bridge and turn left into Alvecote Priory picnic area to view the priory ruins (C).

Re-cross the canal bridge, turn right down a track and pass through a metal barrier to enter the nature reserve. At a fork take the left hand path - not the canal towpath - to continue through attractive woodland, planted on the site of former colliery workings (D). Pass through a metal barrier, keeping on the main path all the time, and eventually bear right through another metal barrier into an open area. Bear left along a wide track, below the partially landscaped coal tip on the left, to rejoin the canal and where the track turns right over bridge 56 descend to the towpath and turn left along it, passing under both bridge 56 and the motorway bridge.

Now comes a relaxing and attractive finale along the tree-lined canal (E), passing the brick-built Pooley Hall above the opposite bank, back to Polesworth. The river is below to the left. After going through a kissing gate, head up to the road at the next bridge and turn left to return to the start.

(A) The much restored church of Polesworth Abbey belonged to a nunnery founded in the 9th century and has Norman arches in the nave, a 14th century tower and a 19th century chancel. The timber-framed Abbey Gateway to the north dates from the 15th century.

Looking across to Alvecote Pools from Shuttington

(B)   This mainly Georgian church is noted for its fine Norman doorway, said to have come from nearby Alvecote Priory.

(C)   Very little is left of this minor Benedictine priory which was founded in 1159 as a cell of Great Malvern Priory and dissolved in 1536. The 14th century ruins now form the focal point of an attractive picnic area and there is a dovecote by the canal.

(D)   Extensive shallow mining, mostly during the Second World War, caused subsidence and led to the River Anker flooding large areas of adjoining land. Now the resulting pools and the woodland around them are a Warwickshire Wildlife Trust nature reserve, a successful reclamation of a formerly ugly area of industrial dereliction.

(E)   Construction of the Coventry Canal, which runs between Coventry and Fradley near Lichfield, began in 1769 and was completed in 1790. Pooley Hall Colliery was sunk alongside it in 1848 in order that the canal could be used for transporting the coal. The mine - later part of North Warwickshire Colliery - closed in 1965 and the canal is now used solely for pleasure cruising.

2. *Kingsbury Water Park*

Route:	Visitor Centre - River Tame - Kingsbury - Visitor Centre
Start:	Kingsbury Water Park Visitor Centre
Distance:	3 miles
Parking:	Visitor Centre
Refreshments:	Cafe at the Visitor Centre
OS Maps:	Landranger 139
	Pathfinder 914

An area of former sand and gravel workings in the Tame valley has been transformed into a delightful 600 acre water park of lakes, small pools, woodland and grassland. This short walk provides you with outstanding views across some of the lakes, pleasant riverside walking beside the Tame,

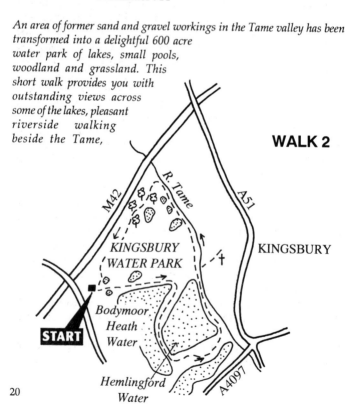

WALK 2

20

attractive woodland, and a short detour to Kingsbury's medieval church, occupying a commanding position above the river and overlooking the park.

(A) With your back to the Visitor Centre, bear left to the corner of the car park, cross a tarmac drive and take the broad, clear path opposite across grass, passing to the right of a pool. Cross a footpath, at a T-junction turn right, in the direction of Kingsbury village, and continue along a pleasant, tree-lined path beside the large expanse of Bodymoor Heath Water on the right.

Take the right hand path at a fork, still in the Kingsbury village direction, and at the next fork, take the right hand path again and cross a footbridge to a T-junction. Turn right along another very attractive, tree-lined path between Bodymoor Heath Water to the right and Hemlingford Water to the left. At the end of the lakes, pass beside a barrier and continue through a car park to a tarmac drive.

Turn left, at a T-junction turn left again, signposted Hemlingford and Mill Pool, and walk along a drive, with Mill Pool to the right, towards the bridge over the River Tame. Just after passing between concrete posts and before reaching the bridge, turn left along a grassy path across the riverside meadows. Continue, beside the river on the right and Hemlingford Water on the left, as far as a footbridge over the river, turn right over it and ascend a flight of steps to Kingsbury church (B).

Return to the bridge, cross it and turn right to resume the walk by the Tame. Soon the bridge that carries the M42 over the valley comes into sight. Immediately after crossing a footbridge over a brook, turn left alongside the brook and follow a grassy track across meadows, later entering trees to reach a T-junction. Turn right, take the first path on the left and continue through attractive woodland.

On emerging into a more open area you arrive at a fork. Take the right hand path across a picnic area to re-enter woodland and continue through it, passing beside a barrier onto a tarmac drive. Cross it, turn right along a path parallel to the drive, and at a fork take the left hand path which curves left across another picnic area to join the path taken near the start of the walk. Turn right and the Visitor Centre is just ahead.

Kingsbury Hall above the River Tame

(A)   Over 50 years of gravel extraction in the Tame valley, plus some imaginative landscaping, has created this highly attractive and popular water park of around 600 acres, particularly desirable in a heavily built up area that lacks natural lakes. There are miles of well-surfaced waterside and woodland footpaths to explore and enjoy.

(B)   This fine medieval church, of Norman origin, was remodelled around 1300 when the tower was built. Adjoining it is Kingsbury Hall, a late medieval fortified house - now a farmhouse - said to occupy the site of a palace of the Anglo-Saxon kings of Mercia.

3. Coleshill and Maxstoke

Route:	Coleshill - Maxstoke Park - Maxstoke - Coleshill
Start:	Coleshill, by the church and war memorial
Distance:	8 miles
Parking:	Coleshill
Refreshments:	Pubs and cafes at Coleshill
OS Maps:	Landrangers 139 and 140
	Pathfinder 935

From the hilltop town of Coleshill, the route descends to cross the River Blythe and continues through pleasant countryside, passing through Maxstoke Park, now a golf course, to reach the hamlet of Maxstoke with its small church and scanty priory ruins. The return leg is mostly along a quiet lane with a short stretch by the River Blythe. This is a walk of expansive views and there is a real feeling of remoteness, despite the proximity of motorways and distant glimpses of the tower blocks of Birmingham on the western horizon.

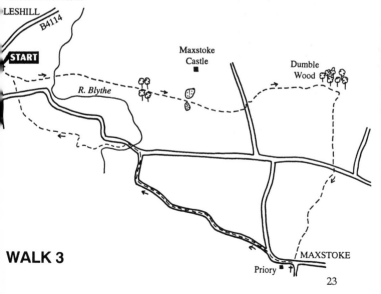

WALK 3

(A) Take the tarmac path that passes in front of the church. Following 'Country Walk' signs, go through an iron gate, bear left and go through a fence gap into a cemetery. Walk across the corner of it, bear right along the edge of the cemetery and turn right through a kissing gate onto a track.

Turn left and after a few yards, turn right through another kissing gate and walk diagonally across a field to a stile. Climb it, bear left and continue gently downhill, curving right to a kissing gate in the field corner. Go through, keep ahead to cross a footbridge over the River Blythe and continue along an enclosed path, which later widens into a track. Keep along this straight track to a stile on the edge of Birch Wood.

Climb it and keep ahead along the right edge of the golf course that now occupies Maxstoke Park. Through the trees to the left the walls of Maxstoke Castle can be seen (B). Continue across an attractive, tree-lined causeway between two lakes, keep ahead across the golf course to a stile, climb it and walk along the left edge of a field. Look out for a stile in the hedge on the left, climb it and head across a corner of the golf course to climb another stile into a lane.

Turn left, turn right along a concrete farm track and about 100 yards before reaching the farm buildings, turn left over a stile. Turn half-right, walk diagonally across a field and climb a stile on the edge of Dumble Wood. Bear right to keep alongside the edge of the wood and in the field corner do not climb the stile but turn right to continue along the field edge. To the right Coleshill church spire can be seen in the distance, and beyond that the tower blocks of Birmingham. Climb two stiles in quick succession, keep along the left edge of a field, climb another stile and continue along the right edge of the next field to yet another.

Climb it, turn left along the left field edge, follow it to the right and go through a gate. Walk along a path, climb a stile, continue along a narrow path and turn right over another stile. Turn left, continue along the edge of a field and go through another gate onto a lane. Turn left, pass in front of a farm, turn right over a stile and walk along the right edge of a field. Go through a gate, turn right along the right field edge, follow it to the left and continue to a stile.

Climb it, pass through a narrow thicket into the next field and continue along its right edge. Maxstoke church and the priory ruins can be seen ahead. Climb a stile, cross a plank footbridge, keep along the right edge of a field, pass through a gap and continue, emerging onto a road opposite Maxstoke church (C). Turn right, pass the priory ruins, follow the road around a right bend and turn left along Arnolds Lane.

Keep along this quiet, pleasant lane for 1¹/₂ miles, eventually reaching a T-junction. Turn left, cross the bridge over the River Blythe and immediately turn left over a stile onto a riverside path. The path later keeps along the left edge of a field and in the field corner keep ahead through a belt of trees to a stile. Climb it, continue along the left edge of the next field, climb another stile and bear right across the next field, making for a hedge corner. The right of way bears left here to continue alongside a hedge on the left to a gate in the field corner. Do not go through the gate but turn sharp right and head back across the field to a pond surrounded by a circle of trees. Follow the curve of the trees to the left, then turn right alongside a line of trees on the left, go through a gap to the right of a section of wall and bear right to climb a stile.

Turn left along the left edge of a field and before reaching the corner, bear right and head across to a stile. Climb it, keep along the right edge of the next field and turn right over a stile in the field corner. Keep along the left edge of a field, turn left over a stile, bear right across the next field and climb a stile onto a track. Turn right to a road, continue along the track opposite and go through a kissing gate into the cemetery. Turn left through a fence gap onto a tarmac path and follow it back to the start.

(A)   On its western side Coleshill overlooks Birmingham and the M42, but to the east of this hilltop town stretches quiet and unspoilt countryside. The town is dominated by the soaring tower and spire of its grand, mainly 14th century medieval church, a landmark for miles around. Some elegant, redbrick Georgian houses remain as a testament to Coleshill's heyday as an important coaching centre on the main route between London and Chester.

(B)   Maxstoke Castle, a 14th century, moated, fortified manor house founded by William de Clinton, lies about 1¹/₂ miles away from the small village of Maxstoke and the priory ruins. Its former deer park is now a golf course and the castle is not open to the public. (C) The Augustinian priory of Maxstoke was also founded by William de Clinton and its meagre and rather precarious looking remains, not open to the public, are incorporated into farm buildings. Although of medieval origin, the small church is mostly Georgian with a Victorian bell turret.

4. *Hartshill Hayes and the Coventry Canal*

Route:	Hartshill Hayes Country Park - Coventry Canal - Hartshill Green - Hartshill Hayes Country Park
Start:	Hartshill Hayes Country Park Visitor Centre
Distance:	4 miles
Parking:	Hartshill Hayes Country Park
Refreshments:	Light refreshments (peak times only) at Visitor Centre, pub at Hartshill Green
OS Maps:	Landranger 140
	Pathfinder 914

The start of the walk is one of the finest viewpoints in Warwickshire, extending across the wide Anker valley to the distant heights of Charnwood Forest in neighbouring Leicestershire and even to the edge of the Peak District. From here the route descends through St Lawrence's Wood to the towpath of the Coventry Canal and follows a pleasant stretch of the canal, before climbing through the beautiful woodland of The Hayes, reputed to be an outlying remnant of the old Forest of Arden, to regain the ridge at the start.

(A) In the far corner of the car park, pass beside a metal barrier to a notice which states 'St Lawrence's Walk Starts Here' and take the path through the trees. You soon emerge from them and keep along the top edge of a sloping meadow, below a reservoir embankment on the left. To the right is the superb view over the Anker valley.

Follow the top edge of the meadow as it curves left to a track and turn sharp right along it, heading downhill into St Lawrence's Wood. At a fork continue along the right hand track downhill through the trees and, at the bottom, do not follow the broad track to the right but keep ahead through a fence gap and after a few yards, turn right along the right edge of a field. Follow the field edge to the left and look out for where the path bears right through a gap and continues as an enclosed path.

At a fence corner turn right uphill along an enclosed path, head over the brow - Mancetter Quarries are over to the left - and later the path bears left and descends to a farm. Go through a gate, walk past the farm buildings to a lane and turn right. After crossing a canal bridge, turn sharp right down to the towpath of the Coventry Canal and turn left along it (B).

Keep along the attractive towpath for 1 mile, passing under three bridges, and at the third (no.33) turn left beside it up to some steps. Turn left over a stile to cross the bridge and take the path straight ahead across a field to emerge onto a track. Climb the steps

WALK 4

Coventry Canal

St Lawrence's
Wood

The
Hayes

HARTSHILL
GREEN

START

HARTSHILL
HAYES COUNTRY
PARK

A tranquil scene on the Coventry Canal near Hartshill Green

opposite and continue between garden fences to a road in a modern housing area. At a waymarked post keep ahead across a grassy area, bear left to another waymarked post and bear right along the main road into Hartshill Green.

Opposite the Stag and Pheasant, turn sharp right along Trentham Road. After a few yards turn left, at a public footpath sign, along a tarmac track and pass beside a barrier. Descend a flight of steps, at the bottom continue along a concrete path raised above the surrounding marshy ground and pass beside another barrier to enter the woodland of The Hayes.

Ascend steps and follow an undulating path through this very attractive woodland, taking care to keep on the main path all the while and ignoring all side paths. After crossing a footbridge over a brook, the path climbs to reach a T-junction. Turn right along a track which bears left and continues to the edge of the wood. Ignoring a stile on the right, keep along the right inside edge of the wood, pass through a fence gap, turn left uphill and follow the path back to the Visitor Centre.

(A) Hartshill Hayes Country Park, comprising 136 acres of open hilltop and woodland, occupies a ridge overlooking the Anker valley. The valley has always been an important routeway and through it passes the A5, on the line of the old Roman Watling Street, the main west coast railway line between London and Scotland, and the Coventry Canal. Both St Lawrence's Wood and The Hayes are mixed woodlands and provide fine walking; the latter is reputed to be a remnant of the Forest of Arden.

(B) For details of the Coventry Canal see Walk 1.

FORMER WARWICKSHIRE

By the 1930s, the expansion of both Birmingham and Coventry drew them closer together and threatened to create a vast urban sprawl right across the middle of Warwickshire. It was precisely because of its built-up nature that this area - the two cities plus the commuter belt of Solihull - was incorporated into the metropolitan county of the West Midlands when local government in England was reorganised in 1974.

In this predominantly urban area of lost or former Warwickshire, there is perhaps a surprising amount of open countryside remaining. One of the walks explores the substantial green wedge that still lies between Birmingham and Coventry, passing through the centre of England and giving you the chance to explore one of the most delightful village churches in the Midlands. Another walk is in quiet country to the south-east of Solihull.

The others are both within the boundaries of Birmingham. One is in Sutton Park to the north of the city, as rural a walk as any in the book. As a complete contrast and to provide both interest and variety, the final walk takes you on a fascinating stroll through Birmingham's refurbished city centre.

5. Sutton Park

Route:	Visitor Centre - Longmoor Pool - Ryknild Street - Bracebridge Pool - Blackroot Pool - Keeper's Pool - Visitor Centre
Start:	Sutton Park Visitor Centre, just beyond Town Gate
Distance:	5¹/₂ miles
Parking:	Sutton Park, by the Visitor Centre
Refreshments:	Cafes in Sutton Park
OS Maps:	Landranger 139
	Pathfinder 913

There are times on this walk when you have to pinch yourself as a reminder that you are within the boundaries of Britain's second city. Sutton Park is a real rural oasis, nearly 2500 acres of heath and woodland to the north of Birmingham, that has survived largely unchanged and intact for centuries. The first part of the walk is mainly across open heathland, the last part mostly through thick woodland, and you pass a series of pools, both attractive features of the park's landscape and useful focal points on the route.

(A) From the parking area by the Visitor Centre, turn left along a tarmac drive and at a fork take the right hand drive, passing beside a gate. Continue through woodland, keep ahead at a junction and pass beside another gate, emerging from the trees to a crossroads of tracks.

Keep ahead, pass beside a gate, gently descend and just before reaching Longmoor Pool, turn right onto a sandy path. Walk across grass, bearing slightly right towards a circle of trees, keep to the left of the trees and continue across heathland to a crossroads of paths. Turn left and on meeting a track, turn left along it. Cross a footbridge over a brook, keep ahead to a crossroads of tracks - just before a group of trees and one of the boundary gates of the park - and turn right onto a straight track (B).

Keep along this track, ignoring all side turns, across part of a golf course to where it seems to peter out at a T-junction. Turn right,

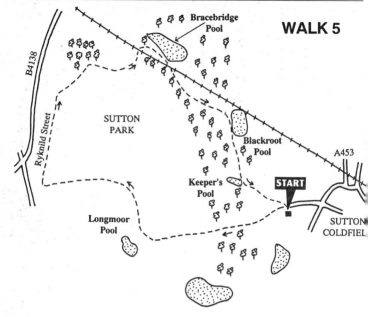

continue along a track across the golf course, pass through a group of trees and keep ahead to a tarmac drive. Turn right and on emerging from the woodland into more open country, turn left onto a wide gravel track, making for the woodland in front.

Pass beside a gate into the trees and after crossing a railway bridge, the track bends left. After a few yards, turn sharp right - almost doubling back - onto a woodland track which later keeps beside Bracebridge Pool (C) to reach a T-junction to the left of another railway bridge. Turn right over this bridge and continue along a track which curves left through more delightful woodland. At a fork shortly after joining another track, take the right hand track which leads to Blackroot Pool.

Continue to the corner of the pool, keep ahead through woodland and pass beside a gate to the edge of Keeper's Pool. Walk across the end of the pool, turn left, pass beside another gate and follow a tarmac drive back to the start.

The scanty remains of Alvecote Priory, now a picnic site (Walk 1)

oking across the Water Park to the tower of Kingsbury church (Walk 2)

The magnificent view over the Anker valley from Hartshill Hayes
Country Park (Walk 4)

In the grounds of Coombe Abbey, now a country park (Walk 10)

(A)   Sutton Park was originally royal forest land and later became a chase belonging to the earls of Warwick. In the 16th century Bishop Vesey, bishop of Exeter and a native of Sutton Coldfield, persuaded Henry VIII to give the lands of Sutton Chase to the people of his home town in perpetuity and this is the reason for its survival as a remnant of genuine open and wild country right on the doorsteps of Birmingham and the Black Country. The only major encroachment in over 400 years was the building of the railway line in 1879 between Birmingham and Walsall, which cuts across the north-east corner of the park.

(B)   This track is on the line of the Roman road of Ryknild or Icknield Street, which ran northwards across the Midlands from Gloucestershire to Derbyshire.

(C)   The various pools in Sutton Park have been around for a long time and were mainly created in order to ensure a regular supply of fish. Bracebridge Pool, often regarded as the most attractive of these, was made for Sir Ralph Bracebridge, who obtained a lease on Sutton Chase from the Earl of Warwick in 1419. Keeper's Pool, passed later on the walk, was also created in the 15th century as a source of fish for the park keeper.

6. Birmingham - Old and New

Route:	Victoria Square - Centenary Square - Gas Street Basin - St Paul's Square - Birmingham Cathedral - New Street - Victoria Square
Start:	Victoria Square
Distance:	3 miles
Parking:	Birmingham city centre
Refreshments:	Pubs, cafes and restaurants in Birmingham city centre
Maps:	Geographers A-Z Street Atlas of Birmingham (Inner City Street Plan) or free Birmingham City Map available from information centres

For those unfamiliar with Britain's second city, this walk, along

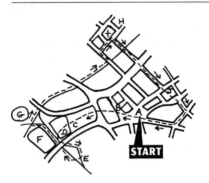

A) Victoria Square
B) Chamberlain Square
C) Centenary Square
D) International Convention Cent[
E) Gas Street Basin
F) Brindley Place
G) National Indoor Arena
H) St Paul's Square
J) Cathedral

WALK 6

pedestrianised streets, through flower-filled squares and by refurbished canalsides, may well come as an agreeable surprise. It takes in some of the new developments around the International Convention Centre, a short stretch of Birmingham's famed canal system, part of the historic Jewellery Quarter, including the city's only remaining Georgian square, and some of the grand Victorian civic building erected when Birmingham was the greatest manufacturing city in the world.

Begin in the recently landscaped Victoria Square, face the Council House and pass between the Council House on the right and the Town Hall on the left into Chamberlain Square (A). Climb the steps beside the Chamberlain Fountain, go through Paradise Forum, along Centenary Way and across Centenary Square to enter the International Convention Centre (B).

If the centre is closed, walk along Broad Street to the left of it and descend steps to the canal.

Otherwise continue through it to emerge onto the canal bank, turn left and pass under Broad Street Tunnel to Gas Street Basin (C). Bear left by an arm of the canal, turn right over a bridge, passing in front of the James Brindley pub, and cross a barrier, the Worcester Bar, between two canals. Cross an iron bridge, walk along the other side of Gas Street Basin and pass under Broad Street Tunnel again. Ahead is the National Indoor Arena.

Pass under a suspension bridge opposite the International Convention Centre and turn left up steps for a brief detour to see the new, award-winning Brindleyplace development (D). Return to the canal, walk past the National Sea Life Centre and cross a bridge to the National Indoor Arena. Turn left in front of it, climb steps and turn right to walk across the terrace above Deep Cutting Junction, a crossroads of canals. From here there is a fine view to the right looking along the canal back towards Gas Street Basin.

At the end of the terrace, descend steps to rejoin the canal and continue along it, passing under Tindal Bridge to Cambrian Wharf. Descend by the Farmers Bridge locks, passing under a cast-iron bridge and Saturday Bridge, and at the next bridge turn left up steps to leave the canal and turn left along Newhall Street. To the left is the entrance to the Museum of Science and Industry and to the right is the Assay Office.

Turn right along Charlotte Street into St Paul's Square (E), turn right again down Ludgate Hill, cross the footbridge over Great Charles Street Queensway and continue up Church Street into Colmore Row opposite the cathedral (F). Cross the churchyard (St Philip's Place), keep ahead down Cherry Street to Corporation Street and turn right to New Street.

Turn right again and walk along the pedestrianised New Street back to Victoria Square.

(A)   Victoria Square was redesigned in 1993, making the most of its sloping position, with new sculptures and a cascading fountain. Around it and the adjoining Chamberlain Square are grouped the major monuments to Birmingham's 19th century greatness: the Town Hall, built in the style of a Roman temple and opened in 1834, the Renaissance-style Council House, dating from the 1870s, and the Museum and Art Gallery, opened in 1885. In the middle of Chamberlain Square is a fountain erected to honour Joseph Chamberlain who did so much to transform the Victorian city.

(B)   The spacious new Centenary Square was laid out to commemorate Birmingham's centenary as a borough in 1989. Among the buildings lining it are the Hall of Memory and Baskerville House, both built in the interwar period, the Repertory Theatre which dates from the 1960s, and the prestigious International Convention Centre, opened by the Queen in 1991 and incorporating Symphony Hall, alleged to be the most acoustically perfect concert hall in the world.

*The Chamberlain Fountain and the Victorian grandeur of
Birmingham Town Hall*

(C)   Gas Street Basin has been at the hub of Birmingham's extensive canal network since the 18th century. Once a bustling centre of commercial activity, it is now the focal point of an area of pubs, clubs, restaurants and wine bars. The Worcester Bar separated two canal systems, the Birmingham Canal Navigations and the Worcester and Birmingham Canal, but a lock was built in 1815 to allow passage from one to the other.

(D)   Brindleyplace is the latest, and as yet uncompleted, phase of the redevelopment of this part of the city, an ambitious scheme that includes a square, fountains, office buildings, restaurants, pubs, gallery and theatre. One part opened in 1996 is the futuristic National Sea Life Centre, situated by the canal.

(E)   St Paul's Square is Birmingham's only remaining Georgian square and is the gateway to the city's historic Jewellery Quarter. In the middle of it stands St Paul's church, built in 1779 and known as the 'jewellers church'.

(F)   An elegant early 18th century church, designed by Thomas Archer, it became the cathedral of the new diocese of Birmingham in 1905.

7. *Berkswell and Meriden*

Route:	Berkswell - Meriden - Meriden church - Berkswell
Start:	Berkswell, by the triangular village green
Distance:	7$^{1}/_{2}$ miles
Parking:	Berkswell
Refreshments:	Pub at Berkswell, pubs and cafe at Meriden
OS Maps:	Landrangers 139 and 140
	Pathfinders 935 and 955

Although in the heart of the West Midlands, and indeed the very centre of England - bordered by Birmingham, Solihull and the M42 to the west, Coventry to the east and the M6 to the north - this walk takes you through a remarkably peaceful and traditional landscape of farmland, parkland and woodland. The only contact with modern industry comes just before reaching Meriden where the route passes close to quarry workings and sand and gravel pits. Despite suburban expansion, both Berkswell and Meriden have managed to retain their village atmosphere, especially the former which has probably the finest Norman church in the Midlands.

(A) Facing the church, walk along Church Lane by the right side of the small triangular green, enter the churchyard, pass to the left of the church and continue to a kissing gate. Go through, keep ahead through a belt of trees, go through another kissing gate and walk along the right edge of a field. Continue along a wooden raised path, cross a footbridge over a brook, keep ahead through woodland and go through a kissing gate.

Immediately turn right through another onto a path, by a fence on the right, that later heads across a field towards trees. To the right the view across the landscaped parkland and lake to Berkswell Hall (1820) is particularly attractive. Climb a stile, keep ahead through the trees, continue along the right edge of two fields and about halfway along the second field, the path bears left to keep along the left inside edge of the mainly coniferous Sixteen Acre Wood. Pass to the right of a small pool, continue through the wood, climb a stile on the edge of it and walk along the left edge of a field.

WALK 7

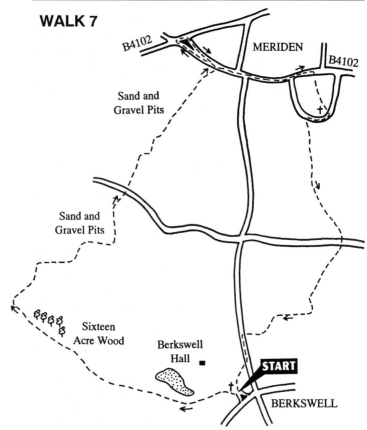

Just before reaching a farm, turn right, at a public footpath sign, and keep alongside an old and interrupted hedgeline on the left to climb a stile in the field corner. Bear right, climb a stile in a wire fence, keep ahead to cross a footbridge over a brook and continue across the next field. Climb another stile, cross a plank footbridge and continue, by a wire fence on the right, to a tarmac track. The next part of the walk is mainly along the right edge of quarry workings and sand pits.

Turn right along the track, follow it round left and right bends and look out for a waymarked stile on the left. Climb it, walk along a narrow path along the right edge of a field and climb another stile. Turn right and the path bends first to the left, then right, left again and finally right again, to emerge via a gate onto a road. Turn right, at a yellow waymark turn left over a stile and walk along a path, between a fence bordering the quarry on the left and a hedgeline on the right - later it keeps below an embankment on the right. Cross a footbridge over a ditch, turn right through trees and in front of a wire fence, turn left and head gently uphill.

Look out for where you turn right over a stile - here leaving the quarry workings - bear left and head diagonally across a large field, descending gently to a stile in the far corner. Climb it, walk across the corner of a field to climb another, cross a footbridge over a ditch and continue in the same direction, making for a stile in the far field corner. Climb it, walk along an enclosed path to a tarmac drive and turn left to emerge onto a road in Meriden opposite the Bulls Head.

Turn left along the road for $1/4$ mile to the triangular green in the village centre (B). Retrace your steps to the Bulls Head and continue past it, passing a pool on the right beyond which is the early 18th century Meriden Hall. Opposite the Queens Head turn right through a kissing gate, at a public footpath sign, and walk along an enclosed path to another kissing gate.

Go through and keep along the left edge of two fields, going through kissing gates, to enter Meriden churchyard. Pass to the left of the church (C), go through a gate onto a lane and turn right. Just before the lane bends right, turn left through a gap between gate and hedge and follow a path across a field, making for a public footpath sign at its left edge. Continue alongside the hedge, climb a stile, keep by the left edge of the next field, climb another stile and bear left across a field corner to climb another stile.

Keep along the left edge of a field, go through a gate, climb a stile, bear slightly left across a field to climb another and continue along the left edge of the next field to a stile in the corner. Walk along a hedge-lined track to a road and go through the gate opposite. Follow a track along the left edge of the first field, then by the right edge of the next two fields, and climb a half-hidden stile in the corner of the last field. Keep along the right edge of the next field, passing to the right of a small pool, follow the field edge to the left and turn right over a stile in the corner. Continue along a track, going through a gate beside a cattle grid and passing to the left of a lovely old brick and half-timbered farmhouse, to a road.

Turn left, look out for a kissing gate in the trees on the right, go through it and continue through the trees to a stile. Climb it, bear left along the left edge of a field - Berkswell Hall is to the right - climb a stile and go through a kissing gate into Berkswell churchyard. Keep along the left edge of the churchyard and go through a kissing gate to return to the start.

(A)   Berkswell is an attractive and remarkably unspoilt village with old cottages grouped around a small green. The church is most unusual and interesting, a rare example of a Norman village church that has survived almost intact. It is particularly noted for its chancel, well-preserved 12th century crypt and the picturesque, timber-framed and two-storied south porch built in the 16th century.

(B)   The cross on the wide, triangular green in Meriden is traditionally regarded as marking the centre of England. Near it is a memorial to cyclists killed in both world wars.

(C)   Meriden's medieval church is isolated because the village moved away from this original hilltop site to be closer to the main lines of communication.

8. *Knowle and Temple Balsall*

Route:	Knowle - Temple Balsall - Grand Union Canal - Knowle
Start:	Knowle, by the church
Distance:	7 miles
Parking:	Knowle
Refreshments:	Pubs and cafes at Knowle, two pubs beside the canal
OS Maps:	Landranger 139
	Pathfinders 954 and 955

From the pleasant commuter village of Knowle, the route heads through tranquil countryside, across fields, along quiet lanes and finally down an attractive, enclosed track to Temple Balsall. After passing the almshouses and church there, it continues via tracks and field paths to the Grand Union Canal. The canal towpath is then followed back to the start, passing the Knowle Locks.

(A) Begin by walking along Kenilworth Road and turn left into Kixley Lane, which soon emerges into open country. Curve right to cross a canal bridge and where the lane ends, keep ahead along a path to a stile. Climb it, cross a plank footbridge, bear right across a field and climb another stile. Continue along the right edge of a field and climb a stile onto a lane.

Turn left and follow this winding lane for ³/₄ mile, crossing a footbridge over the River Blythe by a ford and continuing to a T-junction. Turn right along a tree-lined tarmac track and just before it ends by a house, turn left along a hedge-lined track and follow it to a ford over the River Blythe. Cross a footbridge by the ford and keep ahead to a road.

Turn right into Temple Balsall, take the road on the left, signposted to Fen End and Honiley, and just after passing a school on the right, turn right onto a tarmac path (The Breadwalk), signposted 'St Mary's Church, Lady Katherine Leveson Hospital and Old Hall' (B). The path keeps to the left of the almshouses and

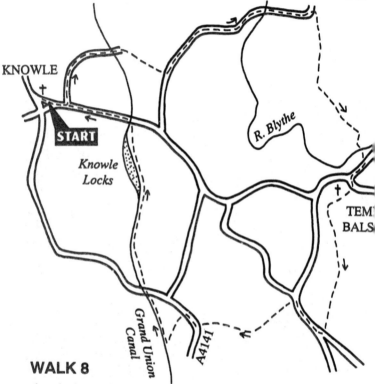

WALK 8

church, descends to cross a footbridge over a brook and continues to a gate and T-junction of paths.

Turn left through a kissing gate, walk along a path to a track and bear right along it. Pass through a gap into a field and keep along its left edge to a stile in the corner. Climb it, turn right along a lane, bear right at a junction just ahead and at a public footpath sign just before a fork, turn sharp left along a tarmac drive towards a house. Pass between the house and garage, go through a gap at a waymarked fence and continue along an enclosed path, gently descending to a kissing gate. Go through, keep ahead to a track and turn right onto it.

Lady Katherine Leveson Hospital -
dignified, late 17th century almshouses at Temple Balsall

Where the track turns right, keep ahead through a gate and walk along an enclosed path. Just before reaching a house, turn left through a gate, turn right and continue along a narrow enclosed path to a gate. Go through, turn right along the main road and at Heronfield Cottages, turn left over a stile and walk along a tarmac track between cottages. Go through a gate, keep along the right edge of a field, turn left in the field corner and continue along the field edge to a stile. Climb it, keep ahead to climb another, continue along a tree-lined path and go through a gate into the yard of the Black Boy.

Turn left into the pub car park, turn right in front of the entrance and turn right again to descend to the Grand Union Canal (C). Bear right onto the towpath and follow it to the second road bridge. Before reaching that bridge, the towpath ascends beside the Knowle Locks, a flight of five locks in only $1/4$ mile. At the bridge, climb up to the road, turn left over the bridge and follow the road back to Knowle.

(A)   Despite recent commuter development, Knowle retains its village atmosphere and many old brick and timber-framed buildings in the High Street. Two of the most prominent of these is the 15th century Chester House, now used as a library, with a Tudor knot garden at the back, and the Guild House to the west of the church. The church, which dates from 1402, is a fine example of the Perpendicular style.

(B)   The interesting collection of buildings along The Breadwalk at Temple Balsall begins with the Lady Katherine Leveson Hospital, a handsome group of almshouses founded in the 1670s and ranged around a quadrangle. Next comes the spacious sandstone church, originally a chapel built either by the Knights Templars, a semi-military religious order founded to protect pilgrims in the Holy Land, or their successors the Knights Hospitallers, who succeeded to their properties after the Templars were dissolved in the early 14th century. After the Hospitallers themselves were dissolved in 1540 the chapel fell into ruin. It was partially restored in the 17th century but its present appearance is mainly the result of a thoroughgoing restoration carried out in the 1840s by the famous Victorian architect, George Gilbert Scott.

(C)   The canal was originally built in 1800 as the Warwick and Birmingham Canal and became part of the Grand Union Canal after eleven different canal companies amalgamated in 1929.

EAST WARWICKSHIRE

Sweeping eastwards and south-eastwards from the edge of Coventry are the wide and extensive vistas of East Warwickshire. This is basically the area that lies between the A423 Coventry-Banbury road and the borders of Leicestershire and Northamptonshire.

Much of the landscape is reminiscent of the neighbouring East Midland counties and is mostly flat or gently undulating, although there are some hills in the south bordering on the Northamptonshire Uplands. This is perhaps the least known part of Warwickshire but should not be neglected as there is much pleasant countryside and some fine walking. Through it flows the infant River Avon which passes to the north of Rugby, the main town of this region.

Two of the walks are in the countryside lying to the north-west of Rugby and utilise stretches of the Oxford Canal, an attractive waterway that runs between Oxford and Coventry. Another is based on a popular and interesting country park on the outskirts of Coventry. The final walk, that starts in the appropriately named village of Napton on the Hill, is in the hillier south of the area and also includes a stretch of the Oxford Canal.

9. *Brinklow and Easenhall*

Route:	Brinklow - Oxford Canal - Easenhall - Newbold Revel - Brinklow
Start:	Brinklow, in the main street opposite The Raven pub
Distance:	6$^{1}/_{2}$ miles
Parking:	Roadside parking in Brinklow
Refreshments:	Pubs and cafe at Brinklow, pub at Easenhall
OS Maps:	Landranger 140
	Pathfinders 936 and 956

After passing alongside the earthworks of Brinklow's motte and bailey castle, there follows a pleasant 1$^{1}/_{2}$ mile ramble along the shady towpath of the Oxford Canal. The route then heads across fields and through woodland into the village of Easenhall, and continues on to the imposing mansion of Newbold Revel. The last stretch takes you across fields and finally under an aqueduct to return to Brinklow.

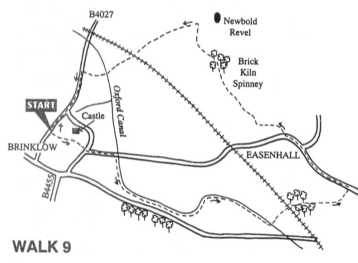

WALK 9

(A) Start by taking the track to the side of The Raven pub - Town Yard - continue along an enclosed path and climb a stile. Turn right over another one, bear left to keep beside the outer ditch of the motte and bailey castle, climb a stile and continue along the left edge of a field. At a hedge corner, bear slightly right and head across the field to climb a stile onto a road by a junction.

Keep ahead along the lane signposted to Easenhall and at the canal bridge, descend steps to the towpath and turn right along it. Now comes an attractive 1½ mile walk beside the Oxford Canal, sometimes tree-lined and at other times with extensive views across the fields on both sides (B). At the third bridge (no 38), pass under it, turn right through a hedge gap up to a path and turn right again over the bridge. Continue along an enclosed, tree- and hedge-lined path, go under a railway bridge and at a fork immediately ahead, take the right hand path through the pleasant woodland of Cathiron Spinneys. Go through a gate to emerge from the trees, continue along an enclosed track, passing through several gates, and on reaching a lane, turn left and follow it into Easenhall.

Walk thorough the village, a mixture of old cottages and modern housing, and where the lane bends left, keep ahead along Farm Lane, signposted 'Bridleroad to Stretton under Fosse'. Look out for a yellow arrow which directs you to turn left through a metal gate and walk along the right edge of Easenhall cricket field to a waymarked post. Bear right along a track, turn left in front of a gate to continue along the right edge of a field and turn right at a fence corner. Keep ahead through a gap and continue along the right edge of a field, following it as it bends left and keeping by a wire fence on the right all the while. Later join a track and continue across fields towards Brick Kiln Spinney.

Take the path through the wood and on the far side continue along a broad, fence-lined track. To the right across sports fields are the lakes and large house of Newbold Revel (C). At a fork and public bridleway sign, take the left hand enclosed track and on reaching the tarmac drive to the house, turn sharp left through a gate, turn right and continue along a narrow path by the left edge of a field. For the rest of the walk you keep alongside Smite Brook on the left.

Follow the meandering field edges to the canal embankment, negotiating a kissing gate and stiles and passing under a railway bridge. In the field corner below the embankment, bear left and then right to cross a footbridge, pass under an aqueduct and continue through a group of trees to a stile. Climb it, keep along the left edge of a field, turn left to cross a footbridge over the brook and turn right along the right edge of a field. In the far corner, keep ahead through trees, climb a stile and turn left along the road into Brinklow.

(A)   Brinklow has a long main street, with some particularly attractive houses and cottages in The Crescent opposite the mainly 15th century church. The mound and extensive earthworks beyond the church are all that remains of a 12th century motte and bailey castle, built by the Mowbrays to guard the Fosse Way.

(B)   The Oxford Canal, built by James Brindley, was the first to provide a link between the River Thames and the industrial Midlands. It was started in 1769 but financial problems delayed its completion until 1790. The Oxford Canal Walk runs along its entire length, approximately 83 miles, between Oxford and Hawkesbury Junction where it joins the Coventry Canal just north of Coventry.

(C)   The large mansion of Newbold Revel was built in 1716 on the site of an old manor house. It is now a training college for the prison service.

10. *Coombe Abbey and Birchley Wood*

Route:	Coombe Abbey Country Park - Birchley Wood - Twelve O'Clock Ride - Coombe Abbey Country Park
Start:	Coombe Abbey Country Park, west side of car park
Distance:	5$^{1}/_{2}$ miles
Parking:	Coombe Abbey Country Park
Refreshments:	Cafe at Country Park Visitor Centre
OS Maps:	Landranger 140
	Pathfinders 935, 936 and 956

WALK 10

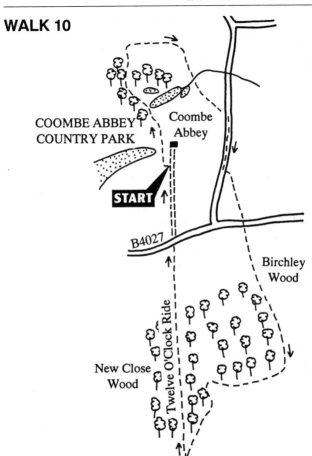

COOMBE ABBEY
COUNTRY PARK

Coombe
Abbey

START

B4027

Birchley
Wood

Twelve O'Clock Ride

New Close
Wood

Coombe Abbey Country Park lies just to the east of Coventry and was created from the parkland of a large house that was itself built on the site of the wealthiest medieval monastery in Warwickshire. Thus it illustrates the many and varied uses of this piece of land over many centuries of continuous occupation. After exploring part of the landscaped park, the route heads across fields and through woodland, and the last part is along a straight drive, Twelve O'Clock Ride, that is aligned with the abbey and leads directly back to the start.

(A) Take the path that crosses the main drive to Coombe Abbey to the new, Classical-designed Visitor Centre, and turn right to pass either to the right or left of it. Continue along the path ahead, cross a bridge over the end of the lake and keep ahead, by water on the left, through the arboretum.

At a T-junction turn left, keep ahead at a crossroads and after crossing a bridge, turn right, at a Centenary Way post, to continue through the woodland, following the Centenary Way marker posts. The path bears left to reach a kissing gate on the edge of the trees. Go through, continue first along an enclosed path and then along the right edge of fields, and at a crossroads go through another kissing gate and turn right onto a track.

The track curves right, passes through Hillfields Farm, then bends left and continues between the buildings of the Rolls Royce works over to the left and the woodlands of Coombe Abbey across the fields to the right. At the end of a hedgeline on the left and just where the track bears slightly left, turn right and follow a clearly discernible path across a field. Go through a fence gap, continue across the corner of a field to climb a stile, cross two footbridges in quick succession and walk across the field ahead, veering left and making for the far corner where you climb a stile onto a road.

Turn right, after 1/4 mile turn left through a gate onto a track and after a few yards, turn right and head across a field towards a belt of trees, making for a blue waymarked post on the far side. Continue through the trees to a road, cross over and continue along the track opposite to Birchley Farm. Keep in a straight line - initially along the left edge of a field, later along the edge of Birchley Wood - and where the track turns left to the farm, continue along the path ahead. In the field corner turn right through a gate to enter the wood, follow the path as it bears left, go through another gate and turn right to continue again along the left edge of Birchley Wood.

Follow the edge of the wood to the left, turn right through a gate in front of farm buildings, walk along the right edge of a field and follow the field edge to the left. In the next field corner go through a gate and turn right along a track. Through the trees on the left is

In the grounds of Coombe Abbey, now a country park

Coventry Stadium. A few yards before the track bears right, turn sharp right, pass beside a gate and walk along a straight path through the very attractive New Close Wood.

This is the Twelve O'Clock Ride and you follow it in a straight line back to the start. After going through a gate on the edge of the wood, keep ahead across open country, pass beside a gate onto the road opposite the entrance to the Country Park, continue along the drive towards the abbey and turn right to return to the car park.

(A)   Coombe Abbey and the land around it have certainly had a variety of roles over the centuries. Founded in 1150 as a Cistercian monastery, it became the wealthiest abbey in Warwickshire and was partly responsible for the growth of the wool trade in medieval Coventry. After the dissolution of the monasteries in the 1530s, a house was built on the site which was subsequently extended in the 17th and 18th centuries. In the late 18th century the grounds were landscaped by 'Capability' Brown. Now the house is a hotel and the grounds are a very attractive and popular country park, comprising over 400 acres of gardens, woodland, grassland and lakes.

11. *Newbold-on-Avon and Little Lawford*

Route:	Newbold-on-Avon - Little Lawford - Oxford Canal - Newbold-on-Avon
Start:	Newbold-on-Avon, at crossroads at bottom end of Main Street by the Old Crown Inn
Distance:	4¹/₂ miles
Parking:	Roadside parking in Newbold-on-Avon
Refreshments:	Pubs and cafe at Newbold-on-Avon
OS Maps:	Landranger 140
	Pathfinder 956

This is a pleasant, easy walk in gentle and undulating country just to the north-west of Rugby. The route twice crosses the River Avon and the last 1¹/₂ miles is along the towpath of the Oxford Canal, passing through the Newbold Tunnel.

Begin by walking uphill along Main Street and at a public footpath sign, turn left into the churchyard (A). Bear right to pass in front of the church tower, look out for a stile in the fence on the right, climb it and follow a path across an attractive, tree-studded meadow. Go through a kissing gate, cross a footbridge and continue through scrub and trees to a tarmac track.

Keep ahead along the track but immediately after passing under a railway bridge, bear right off it to go through a kissing gate. Walk across a field, cross a footbridge over the River Avon and continue across the field to a stile. Climb it and continue across the next two fields, climbing another stile, and on the far side of the second field climb a stile onto an enclosed path. After a few yards, turn right along a path between houses to the end of a road on a new housing estate.

Turn left along the road and opposite a small parking area, turn right along another enclosed path between houses. At a fence corner turn left and shortly turn right to a stile. Climb it, walk across a field, cross a footbridge over a ditch and continue across the field to climb a stile in the far right hand corner. Cross a tarmac track, climb the stile opposite, head across a field, climb another stile and turn right

52

along a track.

Go through a gate, continue along the right edge of a field, re-cross the Avon and keep ahead to an abandoned mill. Follow the track around left and right bends and keep ahead to a lane in the hamlet of Little Lawford. Turn left by the hall (B), take the first turning on the right, signposted Harborough Magna, and walk along a narrow, quiet lane, crossing a railway bridge, as far as the canal bridge.

Descend to the towpath of the Oxford Canal (C) and turn right along it back to Newbold-on-Avon, after 1 mile passing through the 412 foot long Newbold Tunnel. Be warned here of the possibility of some large puddles. At bridge 50, bear right up to a road and turn right along it to the start.

(A)   The lower part of Newbold-on-Avon is indistinguishable from suburban Rugby but the older part up the hill still has the atmosphere of a rural village. The handsome hilltop church has an impressive 15th century tower that overlooks the quiet countryside of the Avon valley.

(B)   The 17th century stable block is all that survives from the demolished little Lawford Hall.

(C)   For details of the Oxford Canal see Walk 9.

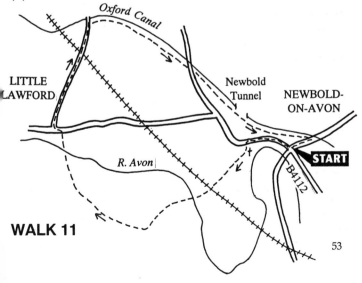

12. *Napton on the Hill and the Shuckburghs*

Route:	Napton on the Hill - Beacon Hill - Upper Shuckburgh - Lower Shuckburgh - Napton Junction - Napton on the Hill
Start:	Napton on the Hill, at the triangular green below the church
Distance:	6 miles
Parking:	Roadside parking in Napton on the Hill
Refreshments:	Pub at Napton on the Hill, pub where you leave the Oxford Canal
OS Maps:	Landranger 151
	Pathfinder 977

This is quite a hilly walk by the standards of east Warwickshire. Napton stands on an abrupt hill, 450 feet above the junction of the Oxford and Grand Union Canals, and to the east the wooded Shuckburgh Hills rise to 675 feet and overlook Shuckburgh Park. After descending from Napton on the Hill, the route passes through the park, linking the isolated church at Upper Shuckburgh with that at Lower Shuckburgh down on the main road, and includes a 2 mile stretch of canal walking before climbing back up to the start.

(A) Facing the triangular green, turn left along School Hill, bear left on joining a lower road and at a public footpath sign by the corner of a building, turn right down steps. Keep ahead to climb a stile and head downhill along the right edge of a field to another one.

Climb that, continue across the next field down to a stile, climb it, cross a track and climb the stile opposite. Walk along the right edge of a field, climb a stile by a waymarked telegraph pole, bear right, head across a field and go through a gate in the corner onto a lane. Turn left and after a few yards, turn right over a stile, head across to climb another and continue across rough grass, passing to the left of a pool. Climb a stile onto a lane, turn right and turn left to cross two stiles in quick succession, and the intervening plank over a ditch.

WALK 12

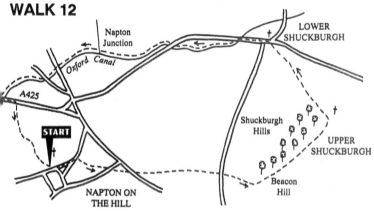

Turn half-right and walk across the corner of a field to a stile, climb it and continue across the next field, later keeping by a hedge on the right. Go through a wide gap in the field corner and keep straight ahead across the next three fields, via a stile and hedge gap, to emerge onto a lane. Turn left and at a public footpath sign, turn right over a stile, walk along the right edge of a field, by a wire fence, and in the field corner turn right over another stile and cross a footbridge over a ditch. Climb a stile, turn left and head up over the Shuckburgh Hills, keeping along the left edge of a field and later by woodland on the left.

In the top corner turn left to climb a stile and continue over Beacon Hill (675 feet) to a field corner where you turn right onto a track. Turn left through a gate, head downhill through Shuckburgh Park, still close to the edge of the wood on the left, pass through a hedge gap and continue down to a gate. The track curves left to a stile: climb it, keep ahead into a hollow and turn left to a kissing gate (B). Go through, keep ahead - still by the edge of the wood - to go through another and continue along the top of a low ridge, with fine views all around and the spire of Lower Shuckburgh church ahead. Climb a stile, descend from the ridge to a fence corner and continue across the sloping field down to a gate. Go through, cross a footbridge over a brook, head across to the field corner and climb a stile onto the road in Lower Shuckburgh opposite the church (C).

Turn left and after crossing the canal bridge, turn sharp right, at an Oxford Canal Walk sign, onto a path which descends to a gate and the canal towpath. Turn right, pass under the bridge and keep beside the canal, passing under another bridge to reach Napton Junction (D). Cross a footbridge over the Grand Union Canal, continue under two more bridges and at the third one, by the Napton Bridge Inn, turn right through a gate in front of the inn and turn left up steps to the road.

Cross the bridge and take the first turning on the right, signposted Napton Industrial Estate. Almost immediately turn left over a stile, at a public footpath sign, and head uphill along the right edge of two fields to a stile in the corner of the second field. Bear left across the next field, climb a stile and continue ahead to climb another one onto a lane on the edge of Napton on the Hill.

Bear left along a sunken, hedge-lined, tarmac track, signposted to 'Village Post Office and Napton Bottom Lock', heading gently downhill, and at a fork continue along the left hand track. On joining a lane, bear left to the start.

(A)   The houses and thatched cottages of Napton cluster around the slopes of the steep hill and command superb views. Around the base winds the Oxford Canal; the north side of the hill overlooks its junction with the Grand Union and on the south is a flight of nine locks. The church appropriately occupies the highest point, a mixture of styles with a Norman chancel, 13th century transepts and a west tower added in the 18th century.

(B)   Almost hidden amongst the trees on the hill to the right is the isolated Upper Shuckburgh church, a 17th century rebuilding of a Norman church with memorials to the Shuckburgh family.

(C)   This flamboyant Victorian church, influenced by oriental designs, is built of yellow stone and has a hexagonal tower. The red-brick arches in the nave are rather startling.

(D)   Napton Junction is where the Oxford and Grand Union Canals separate. For details of the Oxford Canal see Walk 9, and for the Grand Union Canal see Walk 8.

FOREST OF ARDEN

'Well, this is the Forest of Arden!' states Rosalind in *As You Like It*, an indication that this is as much part of Shakespeare Country as Stratford and the Avon valley. In the Middle Ages the forest probably covered most of the county north of the Avon and was itself part of the extensive forest land that extended over much of the Midlands at the time.

For the purpose of this walking guide, the Forest of Arden is confined to the heart of the former forest, an area sandwiched between the West Midlands border to the north and the Avon valley to the south. Although a large area of wood and heath and therefore a forest in the physical sense, Arden was not a forest in the legal sense as it was never a royal hunting ground protected by a special code of laws.

Although the forest has now gone, largely cut down in previous centuries to feed the iron industries of Birmingham and the Black Country, it is still a well-wooded region with some delightful old villages, pleasant towns, lots of attractive Tudor buildings and several idyllic manor houses. The selection of walks illustrate all these features and include two manor houses, woodland and lakes, Arden's main town, a fine hilltop village and one of the grandest medieval castles in the country.

13. Earleswood Lakes

Route:	New Fallings Coppice - Earlswood Lakes - Clowes Wood - New Fallings Coppice
Start:	New Fallings Coppice, Wood Lane car park between Earlswood and Earlswood Station
Distance:	3 miles
Parking:	Wood Lane car park
Refreshments:	None
OS Maps:	Landranger 139
	Pathfinder 954

Earlswood Lakes, a collection of three reservoirs constructed in the early 19th century to supply water to the nearby Stratford-upon-Avon Canal, have now becomes established and attractive features of the landscape in an area lacking in natural lakes. The walk is mainly through the fine woodlands that adjoin part of the lakes, and the combination of woodland and water provides both easy, pleasant walking and a number of outstanding views.

From the car park go through a kissing gate into the woodland of New Fallings Coppice, immediately turn left over a stile and walk along the ridge edge of a field. Just before the field corner, turn right into the trees, at a yellow waymark, follow a path to a fence corner, near a wooden building on the left, and bear slightly right to reach a T-junction.

Turn left, cross a footbridge and turn left again to continue along an attractive, tree-lined path, between a brook on the left and Terry's Pool on the right, that curves right to another T-junction. Turn right over a metal footbridge and walk across a causeway between two of the Earlswood Lakes - Terry's Pool on the right and Engine Pool on the left (A). On the other side, turn right through a gate and follow another tree-lined path along the south side of Terry's Pool, eventually passing between gateposts.

Turn left here, cross a footbridge, climb two stiles in quick succession and walk along the right edge of a field, soon re-entering the trees. Climb a stile in front of a railway embankment, turn left

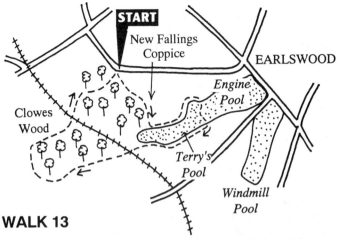

WALK 13

up the embankment, cross the railway line, turn right and descent to climb another stile. Walk across the corner of a field, climb two more stiles in quick succession and continue along the right edge of a series of fields and over several stiles, by the edge of Clowes Wood all the while.

Eventually climb a stile at the corner of the wood, bear right across a field corner, climb another and continue along the left edge of a wood. In the field corner, turn right over the first of two stiles - at a Nature Reserve notice - and follow an attractive path along the left inside edge of Clowes Wood. Turn left over a footbridge, turn right to cross a footbridge over a railway, keep ahead through the wood and bear left to cross a footbridge over a brook. Shortly look out for a fork - by a short, yellow-topped post - and take the right hand path, passing another yellow-topped post, to emerge into a clearing. There is no clear path at this stage but bear right and head slightly downhill, looking out for a footbridge which is the required landmark.

Cross it and from here a broad, clear path leads back to the kissing gate on the edge of the wood at the start. Go through it into the car park.

(A)   Earlswood Lakes comprise the adjacent Terry's Pool, Engine Pool and Windmill Pool, and were constructed in 1810 as feeder reservoirs for the nearby Stratford-upon-Avon Canal. Together with the woodlands to the north and west, New Fallings Coppice and Clowes Wood, they make up a Warwickshire Wildlife Trust nature reserve and are a popular local recreational amenity.

14. Tanworth-in-Arden

Route:	Tanworth-in-Arden - Umberslade Park - Danzey Green - Tanworth-in-Arden
Start:	Tanworth-in-Arden, by the church and Bell Inn
Distance:	5 miles
Parking:	Roadside parking in Tanworth-in-Arden
Refreshments:	Pub at Tanworth-in-Arden
OS Maps:	Landranger 139
	Pathfinders 954 and 975

After descending from the attractive hilltop village of Tanworth-in-Arden, the route first heads along the straight drive of Umberslade Hall and then continues, via a mixture of field paths, tracks and quiet lanes, into the hamlet of Danzey Green. More tracks and field paths lead back to the start, with the spire of Tanworth church acting as a convenient landmark.

(A) Face the church and take the road to the left of it, heading downhill. After crossing a road on the right, bear right onto a straight, tarmac, tree-lined track, signposted to Umberslade Children's Farm, and keep along it for the next 1¼ miles. Soon after passing under a railway bridge, the tarmac drive turns right but at this point keep ahead and the facade of Umberslade Hall comes into view (B).

Climb a stile, turn right along a lane and climb the second stile on the right. Walk along a track, go through a hedge gap, head downhill across a field and veer right near the bottom end to a stile. Climb it, keep along the right edge of a field and at a public footpath sign, turn left and walk across the middle of the field to climb another stile. Keep ahead, pass through a hedge gap and head

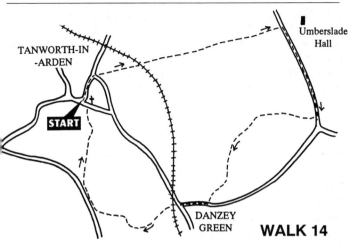

WALK 14

gently uphill to a gate. Go through, bear left, passing to the right of a pool, keep along the left side of the field and go through another gate. Continue to a farm and in front of it, turn left over a stile and turn right along a track, passing to the left of the house. Follow the track downhill to a lane.

Turn right along the lane (Pig Trot Lane) to a T-junction at Danzey Green, turn right and turn left through a gate. Cross a railway bridge, walk along a wide track and at a fork, continue along the right hand track. Over to the left are the slopes of Mockley Wood. Go through a gate, keep along the left edge of a field which curves right to the field corner and turn left through a gap. Continue along the left edge of the next field and then along a concrete track, passing to the right of a barn, to a lane.

Just before the lane, turn right over a stile and head uphill along the left edge of a field, by a hedge on the left and keeping parallel to the lane. About 100 yards before the group of trees ahead, bear right across the field corner, climb a stile and walk along the left edge of a field, by trees on the left. In the field corner turn right along a track and head downhill along the left edge of fields.

At the bottom, bear right to cross a footbridge over a brook, continue uphill along the left edge of a field and climb a stile in the

Umberslade Drive near Tanworth-in-Arden

top corner. Bear left along an enclosed path which emerges onto a road and turn left into Tanworth-in-Arden.

(A)   Grouped around the green in the centre of this hilltop village are attractive old houses, the village inn and a 14th century church. The broach spire of the church is visible from several points on the walk and overlooks a quiet and largely unchanged countryside in the heart of the old Forest of Arden.

(B)   The 18th century hall was the home of Thomas Archer, an architect of some renown. Among the buildings he designed is Birmingham Cathedral.

15. Packwood House and Lapworth Church

Route:	Lapworth - Grand Union Canal - Packwood House - Lapworth church - Stratford-upon-Avon Canal - Lapworth
Start:	Lapworth, picnic area by Stratford Canal, from B4439 (Old Warwick Road) turn along Brome Hall Lane and picnic area is on the left
Distance:	6¹/₂ miles
Parking:	Brome Hall Lane picnic area at Lapworth
Refreshments:	Pub near start, pub by Stratford Canal
OS Maps:	Landranger 139
	Pathfinder 954

The starting point is close to Kingswood Junction where the Grand Union Canal and the Stratford-upon-Avon Canal meet. Both canals are utilised on the walk, which also includes the impressive avenue of Packwood Drive, Packwood House, noted for its Yew Garden, parkland, and the isolated medieval church of Lapworth, all set in a pleasant and typical Arden landscape of gently rolling, wooded countryside.

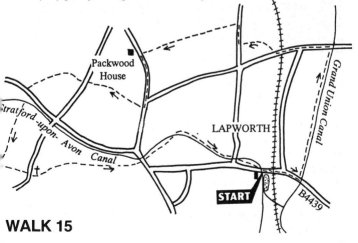

WALK 15

(A) Facing the canal, turn left, pass under bridge 35, head up beside a lock, turn sharp left and left again over the bridge and walk along the road. Go under a railway bridge and in front of the bridge over the Grand Union Canal, turn right down steps and go through a gate onto the towpath. Turn left, pass under bridge 65 and keep along a straight stretch of the canal to the next bridge (no 66).

Turn left, go through a gate onto a road, turn left along it and just past the railway bridge, turn right along a hedge-lined, tarmac drive. In front of gates to a house, bear right along an enclosed path, go through a kissing gate, bear left and continue along an enclosed path to go through another one onto a track. Go through the kissing gate opposite, walk along the left edge of a field and go through a gate onto a road. Turn right and at public footpath and National Trust Packwood Avenue signs, turn left over a stile.

Walk along the length of the impressive, tree-lined Packwood Avenue which leads to the front of Packwood House. Go through gates, descend steps, walk across the grass and turn left along the lane in front of the house, passing the Yew Garden (B). Opposite a road junction, turn right up steps and over a stile, keep along the right edge of a lawn, passing above a pool, and continue along a path, by woodland on the right, to a stile. Climb it, walk along the right edge of a field, climb another stile in the field corner and keep ahead to climb another one. Turn right along the edge of a field, follow it round to the left and climb a stile to enter the parkland adjoining Packwood House. As you proceed along the left edge of the park, passing a waymarked post, there are lovely views to the right across the lake to the back of the house.

Climb a stile onto a lane, take the tarmac drive opposite to Malt House Farm and in front of iron gates, turn left and walk along the right edge of a field, looking out for a stile in the hedge. Climb it, turn left along the left edge of a field, pass through a hedge gap and continue along the right edge of the next field. Where the field narrows, keep ahead and climb a stile onto a road.

Turn left, turn right along the track to Drawbridge Farm, cross the drawbridge over the canal, climb a stile and continue along the track. Pass between the farmhouse and barns to a stile, climb it and walk along the left edge of a field. To the left the spire of Lapworth church comes into view. Go through a gate, head downhill across a

A distant view of Packwood House from across the park (Walk 15)

e motte is all that remains of Beaudesert Castle near Henley-in-Arden, former stronghold of the De Montforts (Walk 16)

The churches at Beaudeseret and Henley-in-Arden can both be
seen from the motte of Beaudesert Castle (Walk 16)
The lovely moated manor house at Baddesley Clinton (Walk 17)

field, climb a stile at the bottom, bear slightly left to keep close to the left edge of the next field and climb a stile in the corner. Continue through a small group of trees and then turn half-right to head uphill to a stile. Do not climb it but turn sharp left to head back downhill across the field, in the direction of the church, and at the bottom cross a footbridge and climb a stile. Walk uphill across the next field, go through a gate, keep ahead and climb a stile onto a lane in front of Lapworth church (C).

Go through a gate and up steps into the churchyard, passing to the right of the porch, continue along a path and go through gates onto a lane. Climb the stile opposite, keep by the left edge of a field, climb another stile, continue along the right edge of fields and in the field corner bear right to a stile. Climb that one, continue across a field, keeping parallel to its right edge, climb another stile and keep along the left edge of the next field.

Where the hedge on the left ends, keep ahead to climb a stile by a fence corner and bear slightly left across the corner of a cricket field to a kissing gate. Go through, walk along the right edge of a field, go through a gap and continue along the right edge of the next field, bearing left to climb a stile in the field corner onto a road. Turn right - not along the road but onto a path that descends to the towpath of the Stratford-upon-Avon Canal (D).

Turn right under bridge 31, walk along the towpath and by some locks, turn left over a bridge and turn right to continue along the left bank. Descend beside the long flight of the Lapworth locks, at the bottom turn right over a bridge and turn left to continue once more along the right bank. After passing under bridge 34, the canal bends right past more locks, and at the next bridge (no 35) head down under it, keep ahead and just before reaching Kingswood Junction, turn right into the car park.

(A)   Just to the south of the starting point is Kingswood Junction, where a short branch links the Stratford-upon-Avon Canal with the Grand Union Canal. For details of the Grand Union Canal see Walk 8.

(B)   The mainly 16th century Packwood House has been much altered over the centuries. It was the home of the Fetherston family who certainly seemed to have hedged their bets during the Civil

War, allegedly providing hospitality both to the Parliamentary General Ireton prior to the battle of Edgehill in 1642, and to Charles II after his defeat at the battle of Worcester in 1651. The famous Yew Garden at the side of the house is meant to symbolise the 'Sermon on the Mount'. The house is now owned by the National Trust and contains a fine collection of 16th century textiles and furniture.

(C)   The medieval church stands some distance from the present village of Lapworth, which grew up on its present site after the building of the canal and railway line. It is a most impressive building, mostly dating from the 14th and 15th centuries, with several unusual features. These include a west porch, and a tower and spire on the north side almost detached from the main body of the church.

(D)   The Stratford-upon-Avon Canal runs through the gentle Warwickshire countryside from King's Norton on the southern outskirts of Birmingham, where it joins the Worcester and Birmingham Canal, to where it empties into the River Avon by the Royal Shakespeare Theatre at Stratford. It was completed in 1816 and after falling into dereliction earlier this century, it was restored and made navigable again from 1964 onwards.

16. *Henley-in-Arden and Lowsonford*

Route:	Henley-in-Arden - Preston Bagot - Stratford-upon-Avon Canal - Lowsonford - Henley-in-Arden
Start:	Henley-in-Arden, in High Street by the church
Distance:	7 miles
Parking:	Henley-in-Arden
Refreshments:	Pubs and cafes at Henley-in-Arden, pub at Lowsonford
OS Maps:	Landranger 151
	Pathfinder 975

You begin by walking below the mound of Beaudesert Castle and take an undulating route across fields, before climbing up to the isolated Preston Bagot church, a fine viewpoint. From there you descend to the Stratford

Canal and follow a most attractive 1 mile stretch of it to Lowsonford. The return to Henley-in-Arden is along part of the well-waymarked Heart of England Way and there is a dramatic finale as you head over the extensive earthworks of the vanished Beaudesert Castle, with Henley and the surrounding Arden countryside spread out before you.

(A) Turn down Beaudesert Lane beside Henley church, cross a bridge over the River Alne, pass Beaudesert church and where the lane turns right in front of the castle mound, (B) keep ahead along an enclosed, tarmac path. The path keeps below the earthworks of the castle and you follow it around right and left bends. Cross the end of a road, keep ahead, still along an enclosed path, turn right by the edge of a school playing field and turn left to a road.

Cross over, take the track ahead, climb a stile and bear left across the corner of a playing field towards trees. Continue steeply uphill through trees and scrub, ascend steps, climb a stile and bear right to climb another. Turn left, walk along the left edge of a field and climb a stile onto a lane. Turn right, after a few yards turn left along a track, climb a stile and keep along the left edge of fields, climbing several more stiles, finally turning right onto an enclosed, tree-lined path.

Look out for where you turn left over a stile and head straight

WALK 16

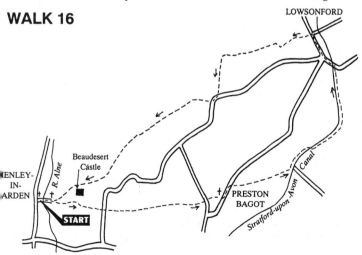

67

across a field to a stile on the far side. Climb it, keep in the same direction across the next field and climb a stile in the left hand corner. Now continue along the left edge of three fields, over a succession of stiles, and on entering the fourth field in the sequence, bear right across the middle of it to a stile. Climb it, descend gently along the left edge of a field to climb another, and continue across the next field. Climb a stile, keep along the left field edge, passing to the right of a barn and black and white cottage, and go through a gate onto a lane.

Cross over, go through a gate opposite and continue along an uphill, enclosed path which curves right to a kissing gate. Go through that, pass to the right of the hilltop, isolated Preston Bagot church (C), a superb viewpoint, and go through another kissing gate onto a narrow lane. Turn left and a few yards after the lane curves left, look out for a half-hidden waymarked stile in a hedge on the right. Climb it, walk along a narrow, hedge-lined path to a stile, climb that and continue along the right edge of a field. Climb a stile in the field corner, keep along the right edge of the next field and just before reaching a brook, turn right over another stile.

Turn left, cross a footbridge over the brook and bear right across a field - likely to be boggy - to go through a gate by a group of trees. Continue in the same direction, by a brook on the right, and in the far narrow corner of the field, climb a stile and go up steps to the towpath of the Stratford-upon-Avon Canal (D) just to the left of a lock and aqueduct. Turn left along it, turn right over a bridge, turn left and continue along the opposite bank of the canal as far as bridge 41.

In front of the bridge bear right through a gate onto a lane, turn left over the bridge, turn right at a T-junction and continue through Lowsonford, passing the Fleur de Lys. Opposite a turning on the right to Rowington and Coventry, turn left along a hedge-lined, tarmac track, joining the Heart of England Way, and where it turns left by a house, climb a stile and walk across a field to climb another. Head gently uphill across the next field, climb a stile, turn right to climb another, immediately turn left over another stile and continue along the left edge of a field, by woodland on the left.

In the field corner climb a stile and continue through the mainly conifer wood, descending and turning left to emerge into a field.

Turn right along the field edge, bear right through a gap in the corner, keep along the left edge of the next field and climb a stile onto a track. Immediately turn left through a gate and continue along a track which curves right and heads across a field to a gate. Go through, turn left onto a tarmac track, cross a bridge over a disused railway and follow the track to a lane.

Turn right and after crossing a bridge over a brook, turn right along a track towards a farm. Just after passing through a hedge gap, bear left across grass to keep beside a hedge on the left and climb a stile in the field corner. Keep ahead along the right edge of a field, climb a stile, bear left across the next field and continue beside its left edge to another stile. Climb it, keep in the same direction across the next field and in the corner continue through a small group of trees to climb a stile. Head across a field to join and bear slightly right along its right edge, continue gently uphill to pass through a gap in the field corner, cross a tarmac track and head straight across the next field, making for a waymarked post in the far left hand corner.

Continue through trees and bushes along an enclosed path which turns left, turn right over a stile, walk across a field, climb a stile in the far corner and bear slightly left to join a track. Bear left along it and now come a series of superb views of the earthworks of Beaudesert Castle, Henley-in-Arden below, and the surrounding countryside. Climb a stile, bear right, head down into a dip and continue up over the castle mound. Finally descend to go through a kissing gate onto a lane and walk along it back to the start.

(A)   The long and attractive main street of Henley-in-Arden is lined with a mixture of brick and half-timbered houses, cottages and inns. Approximately half way along are the church and timber-framed Guildhall, which both date from the 15th century. The large number of inns and eating places is a reflection both of Henley's former importance as a coaching town in the 18th century and its current popularity with local people on a day out.

(B)   Beaudesert church, about three centuries older than the one just up the lane at Henley, is basically Norman apart from the 15th century tower. It is unusual to find two medieval churches so close together but Beaudesert was originally a separate settlement which grew up below the castle of the powerful De Montfort family. After the fall of the De Montforts, Beaudesert declined and became swallowed up by the expanding Henley and only the earthworks remain of the castle, though these are both extensive and impressive.

(C)   This small, isolated Norman church, extensively restored in 1870, has a bell turret at the west end. It occupies a splendid, hilltop position overlooking the countryside of Arden.

(D)   For details of the Stratford-upon-Avon Canal see Walk 15.

17. Hay Wood and Baddesley Clinton

Route:	Hay Wood - Wroxall Abbey - Hay Wood - Baddesley Clinton - Hay Wood
Start:	Forestry Commission picnic site at Hay Wood, off Hay Wood Lane 1 mile south of Baddesley Clinton village
Distance:	4 miles
Parking:	Hay Wood picnic site
Refreshments:	Cafe at Baddesley Clinton Hall
OS Maps:	Landranger 139
	Pathfinder 955

There is a remarkable amount of variety for a walk of such a modest length. It embraces parkland, attractive mixed woodland, some meagre monastic remains, two medieval churches and the chance to visit the picturesque moated manor house of Baddesley Clinton, now owned by the National Trust.

Turn left out of the car park and just after passing a junction on the right, turn left through a metal gate and walk along the left edge of a field. Climb a stile in the hedge on the left and head across a field in the direction of the large, red-brick Victorian house of Wroxall Abbey.

On the far side climb a stile on the right edge of a belt of trees, bear left uphill across parkland to a waymarked post and continue in the same direction, looking out for the next waymarked post on

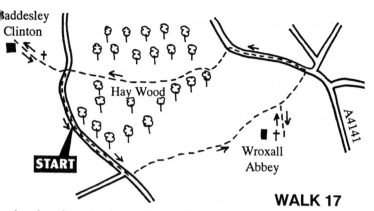

WALK 17

the edge of a circle of trees. Here go through a kissing gate, continue through the trees, go through a kissing gate on the far side, keep ahead across a field, go through another kissing gate and bear left along a track to a waymarked post.

At this point turn right for a brief detour to see Wroxall church and scanty abbey ruins. Walk across the park, parallel to an avenue of trees on the right, go through a kissing gate, continue along a tarmac drive, by a wall on the right, to a crossroads and turn right. Ahead is the Victorian Wroxall Abbey, on either side of the drive are the church and very slight remains of the medieval abbey (A).

Retrace your steps to the track and waymarked post, turn right and follow the track, through a gate and over a stile, to a road. Turn left and after ¹/₂ mile, turn left along the tarmac drive to Wood Corner Farm. Go through a gate, bear left in front of the half-timbered farmhouse along a tarmac drive and turn right along a track, passing to the right of a barn, to a gate. Go through and walk across a field, veering right to go through a gate in the field corner into Hay Wood.

At a fork a few yards ahead, take the left hand track through this attractive area of mixed woodland and at a crossroads keep ahead along the bridleway, which narrows to a path and continues to a gate in front of a cottage. Go through, walk along a drive to a lane and turn left along it.

Now comes another short detour to Baddesley Clinton. At a

The gatehouse of the moated manor house at Baddesley Clinton

The imposing remains of Kenilworth Castle (Walk 18)
Looking across the Arden countryside towards Aston Cantlow
from the edge of Withycombe Wood (Walk 19)

The River Avon at Stratford - looking downstream to the Royal
Shakespeare Theatre and Holy Trinity Church (Walk 22)
Shottery Brook and Anne Hathaway's Cottage (Walk 22)

public bridleway sign, turn right along a tree-lined drive, go through a gate at the end of it, keep ahead and go through a kissing gate into the churchyard. Continue through it, passing to the left of the church (B), go through a gate and walk along a lovely tree-lined path to emerge onto a drive by the entrance to the manor house (C).

Retrace your steps to the lane, turn right and follow it back to Hay Wood picnic site.

(A)   The red-brick Victorian mansion was built in 1866 on the site of an Elizabethan house once owned by Sir Christopher Wren. For many years it was used as a school but is now a conference, health and leisure centre called Wroxall Manor. Of the 12th century Benedictine nunnery, all that survives is two small fragments of the cloister and part of the church. The medieval church is the north aisle of the former abbey, with a brick west tower added in the 17th century.

(B)   Inevitably there are close links between the church and nearby house. The mainly 15th century church was built by Nicholas Brome to atone for the murder of the local priest in 1485, and the chancel was added in the 16th century by the Ferrers family, who inherited the manor house from the Bromes by marriage. Inside are graves and memorials to both families.

(C)   With its walls reflected in the waters of the moat and a bridge leading to a battlemented gatehouse, Baddesley Clinton is everyone's idea of how the perfect medieval manor house should look. The oldest part dates from the 14th century, additions were made over the following centuries and it remains much as it was in the 1630s. Among the items of interest inside are family portraits, priest holes and a chapel.

18. *Kenilworth*

Route:	Kenilworth - Abbey Fields - Kenilworth Castle - Chase Wood - Kenilworth Castle - Abbey Fields - Kenilworth
Start:	Kenilworth, at entrance to Abbey Fields
Distance:	$5^{1}/_{2}$ miles
Parking:	Kenilworth, Abbey Fields car park
Refreshments:	Pubs and cafe at Kenilworth
OS Maps:	Landranger 140
	Pathfinder 955

The first and last parts of this walk are through the pleasant parkland of Abbey Fields that lies between Kenilworth town centre and the castle and contains the scanty remains of an abbey. The rest of the route is across fields and around the edge of Chase Wood, and for much of the way the views are inevitably dominated by the extensive and imposing ruins of the great castle.

Enter Abbey Fields by the car park entrance and take the tarmac path across the park, passing to the left of Kenilworth parish church and, a little further on, the slight remains of the abbey (A). Keep to the right of a swimming pool and follow the path to the left around the end of the building. Do not cross the footbridge over the brook but turn right and walk along a very attractive path, between Finham Brook on the left and a pool on the right, to emerge onto a road.

Turn left to cross a footbridge over the brook and turn right into the castle car park. At the entrance to the castle (B), do not turn right across a footbridge over the former moat but turn half-right along a track which descends to a fence and then bears right, at a waymarked post, to continue towards the castle. Bear left through a kissing gate, follow a path below the castle walls and climb a stile onto a track just to the left of a pink thatched cottage.

Turn left, turn right over a stile, at a public footpath sign, bear left and head diagonally uphill across a field, passing to the left of

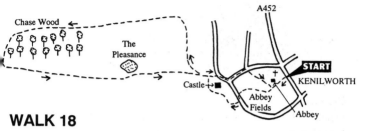

WALK 18

a ruined brick building, to reach a track. Bear right, pass through a gate into a field, walk straight across it, later by the field edge on the left, and climb a stile in the corner. Continue along the right edge of the next field, climb a stile and keep ahead towards farm buildings. Cut across the field corner, keeping to the left of a barn, and on the far side keep ahead along a path, by a hedge on the right, to a stile.

Climb it, turn left onto a tarmac, hedge-lined track (Chase Lane) and keep along it for 1¹/₄ miles. Initially there are wide views across the fields on both sides, later the track keeps along the right edge of Chase Wood. At the corner of the wood, turn left along a broad, gently descending track, initially still by the right edge of the wood but later continuing between fields to reach a crossroads. Turn left, walk along the left edge of three fields, by a hedge on the left all the while, and in the last of these fields comes the first of many superb views of Kenilworth Castle ahead.

Climb a stile in the field corner, keep along the right edge of the next field, climb another stile and cross a track. In the next field veer slightly left away from the edge across the earthworks of The Pleasance, a former pleasure garden, following a visible path which bears right to a stile. Climb it and continue along a narrow, enclosed, tree- and hedge-lined path - later keeping to the left of farm buildings - to join a track. Walk along it and after a slight ascent comes a magnificent view of the castle.

Briefly rejoin the outward route, continue along the track up to a road and keep ahead beside the picturesque cottages of Castle Green. Where the main road curves right, bear left up Castle Hill and at the top, just after passing a thatched, half-timbered cottage, turn right into Abbey Fields. Take the path that bears left downhill

Attractive cottages on Castle Green at Kenilworth

to the abbey remains, turn right down to the swimming pool and turn left to return to the start.

(A) Attractively situated on the north side of Abbey Fields, the most striking feature of the church is the west tower and spire. The nave dates from the 15th century and the elaborate Norman doorway came possibly from the nearby priory. Like the castle, the priory was founded by Geoffrey de Clinton around 1122 and was elevated to the status of an abbey in the 15th century. Little remains apart from a vaulted gatehouse.

(B) Kenilworth Castle, acknowledged as one of the most impressive and substantial ruins in the country, was founded in the early 12th century by Geoffrey de Clinton. Throughout its long and eventful history, it has alternated many times between private and royal ownership. In 1266 it endured a six month siege by Henry III in order to capture it from the powerful and rebellious De Montfort family. Later it passed to the dukes of Lancaster, who succeeded to the throne in 1399, and in 1563 Elizabeth I gave it to her favourite, Robert Dudley, Earl of Leicester. Perhaps the greatest and certainly the most lavish event in its history was when Dudley entertained the queen here for nineteen days in 1575. The existing remains, all constructed from rich red sandstone, belong to three main periods: the powerful 12th century Norman keep, John of Gaunt's banqueting hall built in the 14th century, and Dudley's 16th century gatehouse, part of his ambitious plans to turn the medieval fortress into a grand palatial residence. Some of the surrounding fields over which the walk passes were once lakes that formed an integral part of the castle's defences.

AVON VALLEY

Camden, who travelled around England in the late 16th century, wrote: 'The County of Warwick....is divided into two parts, feldon and woodland or the field and the wooded country, parted from each other by the River Avon running obliquely through the middle of the county'. On its serene journey, Warwickshire's major river flows through beautiful countryside and passes by the two main towns of Warwick and Stratford, as well as a number of idyllic black and white, half-timbered thatched villages.

Shakespeare's presence can be felt throughout the region. He was born, died and spent the greater part of his life in the Avon valley and the area must have inspired many of his writings. Three of the walks have a strong Shakespeare theme. One takes the route from Stratford to Anne Hathaway's Cottage at Shottery that the young William may well have trod in his courting days, another passes two of the villages referred to in a rhyme attributed to him, and the third takes you past his mother's childhood home and the church in which his parents were married.

Two of the other walks have a village theme; the first visits two lovely villages by the Avon, the second takes in three less well-known villages in the tributary valley of the Stour. The final walk enables you to explore the historic county town of Warwick, with is imposing castle, and another stretch of the river.

19. Wilmcote and Aston Cantlow

Route:	Wilmcote - Newnham - Aston Cantlow - Withycombe Wood - Wilmcote
Start:	Wilmcote, by The Green
Distance:	7¹/₂ miles
Parking:	Roadside parking at Wilmcote
Refreshments:	Pubs at Wilmcote, pub at Aston Cantlow
OS Maps:	Landrangers 150 and 151
	Pathfinders 975 and 997

This walk has strong links with both of Shakespeare's parents. The house in which his mother, Mary Arden, lived as a girl is at Wilmcote, and it was in the church at Aston Cantlow that she married John Shakespeare. The outward route is a mainly flat walk across fields; the return leg takes you over two wooded hills, from which there are wide and uninterrupted views over the surrounding countryside of the Avon valley and Forest of Arden.

(A) Start by walking along Aston Cantlow Road and opposite the post office, turn right over a stile, at a public footpath sign, onto a tarmac drive. Where it ends, bear left along a grassy track which becomes an enclosed path, climb a stile, keep ahead to climb another and continue along the right edge of a field.

Climb a stile in the field corner, keep ahead to climb another and now continue in a straight line along the left edge of several fields and over a series of stiles, eventually bearing slightly right across the corner of the last field to climb a stile onto a track. Turn right along it to a lane and turn left through the hamlet of Newnham.

The lane becomes a rough track and a few yards before it bends left, bear slightly right to go through a gate and walk along the left edge of a field. Pass through a hedge gap into the next field, bear left and head downhill to a stile in the bottom corner. Climb it, bear right along the left edge of a field, climb another stile and keep ahead to a lane. Turn left and where the lane bends right, keep ahead through a gate and over a stile and continue along the right edge of two fields, finally turning right along a tarmac track to a road.

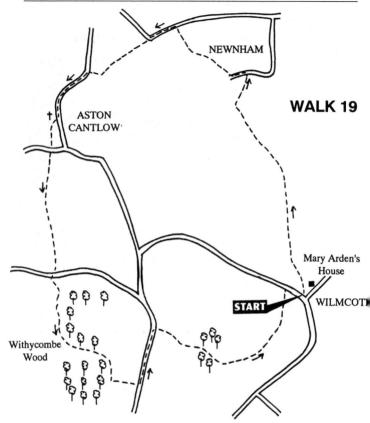

Turn left through Aston Cantlow, turn right by the King's Head along Church Lane and turn left into the churchyard (B). At a fork, take the left hand tarmac path, keeping to the left of the church, climb a stile, walk along an enclosed path and cross a footbridge over a brook. Bear slightly left, head across a field and climb a stile onto a lane. Go through the gate opposite, continue along a track and where it turns right, keep ahead along the right edge of a field, eventually climbing a stile onto a lane.

Turn right, at a yellow waymark turn left through a gate and

Mary Arden's House at Wilmcote, the home of Shakespeare's mother

walk along the right edge of a field. Pass through a gap into the next field, immediately turn left and head gently uphill along its left edge, following the field edge to the right. From here there are fine views to the right across the wide, gentle, well-wooded Arden countryside. The path curves left into trees and then bends right to continue along the right inside edge of Withycombe Wood.

Keep ahead along the bridleway at a waymarked tree and the path now veers left and heads gently uphill through this beautiful woodland. On reaching the edge of the wood, turn right alongside its left edge, bear right through a hedge gap, continue along the edge and at the next hedge gap, turn left along the left edge of a field. Pass to the left of a row of cottages to a lane, turn left and after ¹/₃ mile - where the lane bears left - turn right, at a public bridleway sign, along a track across a narrow field.

The track bears right, becomes tree-lined and where it turns right into a field, keep ahead along a path. This path soon broadens into a track and continues gently uphill through more attractive woodland to a T-junction. Turn right, follow the track to the left, after a few yards turn left over a stile, bear right and head diagonally downhill across a field to a stile.

Climb it, bear right alongside a fence on the right, cross a track and turn left over another stile. Head across a field corner, climb a stile, keep along the right edge of a field, cross a road by a modern housing area and continue along a track into Wilmcote. At a road turn right to the start.

(A)   Mary Arden's House, where Shakespeare's mother was born and lived until her marriage, is a fine example of a large, stone-and timber-built Tudor farmhouse. Some of the original outbuildings survive and now house a museum of local farming and rural life.

(B)   The quiet, attractive village of Aston Cantlow was once a market town but lost out in competition to its larger rivals and the 16th century Guild House, opposite the King's Head, is the only evidence of its former importance. It was in the 15th century church that John Shakespeare married Mary Arden. They went to live in Stratford and William was born in 1564, the third of their ten children but the oldest to survive.

20. *Alcester, Exhall and Wixford*

Route:	Alcester - Oversley Wood - Exhall - Wixford - Alcester
Start:	Alcester, at top of High Street by the church
Distance:	5½ miles
Parking:	Alcester
Refreshments:	Pubs and cafes at Alcester, pubs at Wixford
OS Maps:	Landranger 150
	Pathfinder 997

From Alcester the route heads gently up over Primrose Hill and beside Oversley Wood before descending into the small village of Exhall. It continues along a lane into Wixford and on the final stretch there are fine views across the valley of the River Arrow as you follow the line of the Roman road of Ryknild Street back to Alcester.

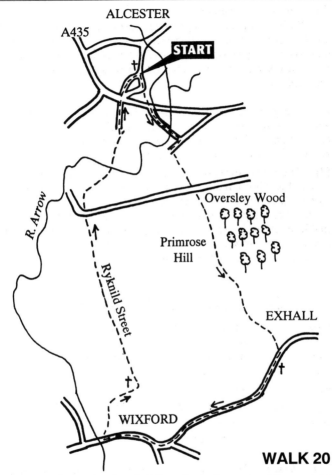

WALK 20

(A) Start by facing the church, follow the main street as it bears right to pass to the right of it and where it bends left, turn right along picturesque Malt Mill Lane. After the lane bends right, turn left, at a yellow waymark, onto a tarmac path across a grassy area to a road.

Cross over, take the lane ahead into Oversley Green, cross a

83

Church and High Street at Alcester

bridge over the River Arrow and at a T-junction turn right along Mill Lane. At a Heart of England Way sign in front of a black and white thatched cottage, turn left along Primrose Lane, turn first right and then left to cross a footbridge over the Alcester bypass and keep ahead to a stile. Do not climb it but turn left downhill along a tarmac track, turn right through a gate at the bottom, cross a tarmac track and keep ahead between hedges to join another tarmac track.

Bear right uphill along it, go through white gates to the right of the gates to a large house and continue along an enclosed path that keeps by the right edge of Oversley Wood to reach a crossroads by the corner of the wood. Keep ahead gently uphill along the left edge of a field and over the rise a grand view unfolds across the Vale of Evesham to the distant line of the Cotswolds. Descend to a stile in the field corner, climb it, turn right to climb another, turn left and head downhill across a field, making for a stile near the bottom left hand corner. Climb it, continue across the corner of a cricket field and walk along a track to a lane in the village of Exhall (B).

Turn right and keep along the lane for 3/4 mile to a T-junction. Turn right and at the next T-junction in front of the Three Horseshoes, turn right again into the village of Wixford. Just before the bridge over the River Arrow, turn right through the car park of the Fish Hotel and go through a gate on the far side. Walk though a small caravan site, below an embankment on the right, keep ahead, climbing two stiles, and the path bears right, passes to the left of a gate and continues in front of a black and white cottage to a crossroads by Wixford church (C).

Turn left along a track - this is on the line of the Roman Ryknild Street (D) - which later continues as an undulating, hedge- and tree-lined path. Cross two tracks and after the second one, the route continues as a broad, grassy, hedge-lined track, with fine views to the left across the Arrow valley to the facade of Ragley Hall. Go through a gate, keep ahead between fences - parallel to the main road - cross the bypass again and continue along a fence-lined path. Turn right through a gate and at a T-junction, turn left onto a tarmac track.

Look out for a public footpath sign where you turn left along a narrow, enclosed path. Cross a bridge over the River Arrow and continue along a tarmac path which becomes a road. Follow it into Alcester and at a crossroads keep ahead along High Street to return to the start.

(A)   There are many attractive corners in Alcester. The High Street has a number of dignified Georgian houses, there is an early 17th century Town Hall, and an outstanding collection of brick and half-timbered cottages in Malt Mill Lane. The town centre is dominated by the church, which from the outside looks a typically late medieval town church, with a fine 14th century tower, but has a Classical interior. This is the result of a rebuilding in 1729-30 following a fire.

(B)   'Piping Pebworth, Dancing Marston
                        Haunted Hillborough, Hungry Grafton,
                        Dodging Exhall, Papist Wixford,
                        Beggarly Broom and Drunken Bidford.'

        Two of the eight villages referred to in this rhyme, allegedly composed by Shakespeare, are visited on this walk. Exhall's description probably stems from its former inaccessibility and it still has a sleepy and off-the-beaten-track feel. The small church has a Norman nave and 13th century chancel.

(C)   Wixford's isolated church has two Norman doorways and a Victorian timber-framed bell turret. It is noted for the fine 15th century brasses on the tomb of Thomas Crewe and his wife.

(D)   For details of Ryknild Street see Walk 5.

21. Two Avon Valley Villages

Route:	Welford-on-Avon - Weston-on-Avon - Welford-on-Avon - River Avon - Welford-on-Avon
Start:	Welford-on-Avon, by maypole and triangular green at south end of village
Distance:	3 miles
Parking:	Roadside parking in Welford-on-Avon
Refreshments:	Pubs at Welford-on-Avon
OS Maps:	Landrangers 150 and 151
	Pathfinder 997

The main attractions of this short walk are the adjacent villages of Welford-on-Avon and Weston-on-Avon, two of the most picturesque in the area, that lie within a loop of the river. Both have a wealth of thatched, black and white cottages, fine medieval churches and attractive riverside locations. Welford is the larger of the two and is well served by pubs. In addition there is pleasant walking by the Avon and some goods views over the valley.

(A) Start by walking along Chapel Lane, turn right for a few yards into Pool Close and turn left onto a narrow, enclosed path. Pass in front of a house, keep ahead and the path widens into a track which continues across fields, bearing first left, then right and finally left again, to a lane in Weston-on-Avon.

Turn right through the small village to see the church (B), retrace your steps and turn right, at a public footpath sign, onto a narrow, hedge-lined path parallel to a lane on the left. Follow this path through trees beside the River Avon to emerge onto a tarmac drive, walk along it for a few yards and turn right along an enclosed path. Bear left to briefly join a parallel drive and then continue along another enclosed path which later keeps along the right edge of a

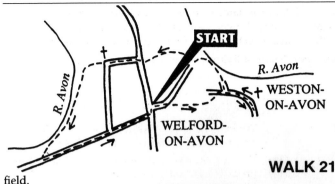

WALK 21

field.

After passing through a gap, follow the waymarked route to the right and left and continue along an enclosed path to reach a road at the north end of Welford-on-Avon. Keep ahead, by a small green, along the attractive Church Street, pass to the left of the church and continue along the equally attractive Boat Lane. Where it ends, keep ahead along a path which bends left, ascends steps and then bends right to a track.

Turn left, after a few yards turn right along a tarmac track which bends right through a small caravan site and where it bends left, bear right to a stile. Climb it, walk along an enclosed path through woodland beside the Avon again, climb another stile and a few yards ahead, turn left up steps. Turn right along an uphill grassy path and at the top, after pausing to admire the view over the valley, turn left through a kissing gate onto a road.

Turn left and walk along the road for just over ¹/2 mile into Welford. At a T-junction, turn left to return to the start.

(A) The idyllic village of Welford-on-Avon has several pubs and a mixture of old and new houses. The maypole on the triangular green, where the walk starts, is the main focal point at the south end of the village. After visiting Weston, the walk passes though the north end of Welford, along picturesque Church Street and Boat Lane where there are many old black and white, thatched cottages. The medieval church has a Norman nave, 14th century chancel and 15th century west tower.

Old cottages at Welford-on-Avon

(B)   Apart from a scattering of newer housing, this small and tranquil village can hardly have changed much since Shakespeare's time. The sturdy 15th century battlemented church overlooks the River Avon.

22. *Stratford-upon-Avon and Shottery*

Route: Stratford-upon-Avon - Shottery - River Avon - Stratford-upon-Avon

Start: Stratford-upon-Avon, by the Shakespeare statue

Distance: $5^{1}/2$ miles

Parking: Stratford-upon-Avon

Refreshments: Pubs, cafes and restaurants at Stratford, pubs and cafes at Shottery

OS Maps: Landranger 151
                  Pathfinders 997 and 998

The walls of Warwick Castle rise majestically above the River Avon
(Walk 24)

Compton Winyates (Walk 26)

The splendid view looking down on Tysoe and the Vale of the
Red Horse from Windmill Hill (Walk 26)
The River Stour near Barcheston

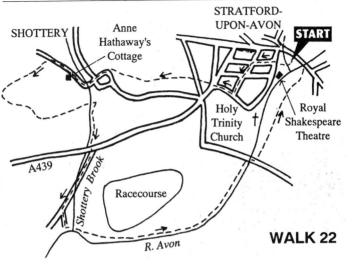

STRATFORD-UPON-AVON

START

SHOTTERY

Anne Hathaway's Cottage

Holy Trinity Church †

Royal Shakespeare Theatre

A439

Shottery Brook

Racecourse

R. Avon

WALK 22

There is very much a Shakespeare theme to this walk. It starts in his birthplace and takes the path across Shottery Fields, now rather built up and suburbanised, to the much photographed cottage which was the family home of his wife, Anne Hathaway. From there it continues to the river and finishes off with a delightful stroll beside the Avon, passing both the church in which he is buried and the Royal Shakespeare Theatre. The walk is short enough to allow plenty of time to visit the numerous Shakespearean properties around Stratford.

(A) From the Shakespeare statue head down to the canal, cross a bridge over it and walk across the riverside gardens, with the Royal Shakespeare Theatre to the left. Cross Waterside, keep ahead along Sheep Street, turn left into Chapel Street and follow it to where it ends. Turn right along Chestnut Walk, cross two roads where they converge and take the tarmac path ahead, signposted to Anne Hathaway's Cottage.

The path keeps in a straight line, crossing several suburban roads and continuing across school playing fields. At a fork take the right hand path, signposted 'Anne Hathaway's Cottage via Tavern Lane' and on reaching the lane keep ahead into Shottery to a crossroads. Bear right, go up steps, through a kissing gate and walk along a path which turns right by Shottery Brook and then turns left over a footbridge onto a lane opposite Anne Hathaway's Cottage. Alternatively if this path is locked - it is not a public right of way - keep ahead at the crossroads along Cottage Lane and follow it to the right to reach the cottage (B).

Turn right along the lane and at a public footpath sign to Hansell Farm, turn left onto a tarmac drive. Head gently uphill, at a left bend turn left through a kissing gate and walk along the right edge of a field, by a fence bordering the drive on the right, to another kissing gate. Go through this, turn left and head downhill across a field. Ahead is a superb view over Stratford and the Avon valley. The path curves right to the bottom corner; keep ahead here through trees and bushes and look out for a left turn beside a redundant kissing gate.

Continue along a tree-lined path back towards Shottery and after crossing a bridge over Shottery Brook, turn right along Hogarth Road. Where the road ends, keep ahead along a tarmac, tree-lined path beside the brook to a main road. Cross over and continue along Luddington Road for nearly ¹/₂ mile, passing the entrance to Stratford Racecourse. Where the road bends right, turn left along Stannells Close and where this ends, turn left along an enclosed track. The track turns right and then left to join the path beside the River Avon.

After crossing a footbridge over Shottery Brook, keep ahead along the edge of lush, riverside meadows, negotiating a series of stiles, gates and footbridges and passing under a disused railway bridge. Immediately after passing under a road bridge, turn right to cross a footbridge over the river and turn left to continue along a tarmac path on the opposite bank.

The last part of the route is particularly attractive as you walk along the edge of a large recreation ground beside the Avon, with grand views across the river of Holy Trinity church and later the Royal Shakespeare Theatre. Finally turn left over the brick Tramway Bridge (C) to return to the Shakespeare statue.

(A)   As the town in which Shakespeare was born, Stratford-upon-Avon is one of the world's major centres of literary pilgrimage and there are many buildings and sites that have links with the playwright

The much photographed Ann Hathaway's Cottage at Shottery

and his family. Foremost among these is the house in Henley Street where he was born in 1564, a mecca for tourists. Others include the Grammar School and adjoining 15th century Guild Chapel where he went to school, the foundations and gardens of New Place where he lived during the latter part of his life and where he died, and Hall's Croft where his daughter Susanna and her husband lived. The beautiful medieval Holy Trinity church, in which he is buried, is situated on the banks of his beloved Avon and upstream is the Royal Shakespeare Theatre, built in 1932 after a fire destroyed its Victorian predecessor.

Leaving aside Shakespeare, Stratford is a highly attractive town in its own right with a superb collection of half-timbered Tudor buildings, splendid riverside gardens and a vast array of shops, pubs, restaurants and tea and coffee houses.

(B)   Many Shakespeare enthusiasts make their way to Shottery, once a rural hamlet but now virtually a suburb of Stratford, to visit Anne Hathaway's Cottage. This half-timbered, thatched farmhouse, a favourite subject for calendars and birthday cards, was the childhood home of Shakespeare's wife. Anne Hathaway was 8 years older than William and they were married in 1582 when he was 18 and she was 26.

(C)   This brick bridge was built in the early 19th century to carry a horse-drawn tramway between Stratford and Moreton-in-Marsh across the River Avon.

23. *Stour Valley Villages*

Route:	Clifford Chambers - Preston-on-Stour - Atherstone-on-Stour - Clifford Chambers
Start:	Clifford Chambers, by church
Distance:	4 miles
Parking:	Roadside parking in Clifford Chambers
Refreshments:	Pub at Clifford Chambers
OS Maps:	Landranger 151
	Pathfinders 997, 998, 1020 and 1021

The River Stour is a tributary of the Avon and the three villages that lie to the south of Stratford-upon-Avon are Clifford Chambers, Preston-on-Stour and Atherstone-on-Stour, all quiet and attractive villages with a definite 'off the beaten track' feel. There are some pleasant and extensive views over both the Avon and Stour valleys from a number of points on the walk.

(A) Walk down towards the end of the main street, passing to the right of the church, and about 50 yards before the gates of a large house, turn right along a grassy track. Turn left at a T-junction, climb a stile and turn right along a straight track. At a fork by a footpath post, take the right hand path which turns left and heads gently uphill along the right edge of a field.

In the top corner follow the field edge first to the left and then to the right, and at the next corner keep ahead through a gap to continue along the left edge of the next field. Pass through a hedge gap on the left, keep in the same direction along the right edge of a field and, with a fine view ahead over the Avon valley, descend to

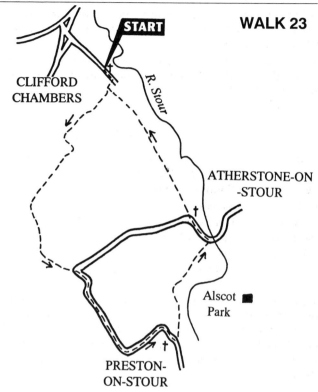

START

CLIFFORD
CHAMBERS

R. Stour

ATHERSTONE-ON
-STOUR

†

Alscot
Park

†

PRESTON-
ON-STOUR

the field corner just to the left of Cold Comfort Farm. Turn left along the bottom edge of the field, bear left through a hedge gap in the corner, turn right and head straight across the next field, making for a stile just to the right of a conifer plantation.

Climb it, turn left along a hedge-lined track, climb another stile, turn left at a T-junction and a few yards ahead, turn right along a narrow lane. Follow this lane around several bends into Preston-on-Stour, finally going round a right bend to reach the spacious green (B). At a T-junction by the war memorial turn sharp left along a lane and where it ends, keep ahead along a path between trees to a kissing gate. Go through, walk across a field and to the right is a

The placid River Stour near Atherstone

grand view of Alscot Park across the Stour valley (C).

Go through a gate, continue along the right edge of a field and in the field corner turn right along a pleasant, winding, enclosed path to reach a lane by a bridge over the River Stour. Turn left into Atherstone-on-Stour and just after the lane bends left by the church (D), turn right along a broad, straight track. Go through a hedge gap into a field and continue across it, passing to the right of a solitary tree and making for a brick building on the far side.

Go through a gate to the left of this building and continue along an enclosed path to a track. Cross it, climb a stile opposite and retrace your steps to the start.

(A)   Clifford Chambers mainly comprises one long, wide street, bordered by a green and lined with a mixture of brick and timber-framed cottages. The medieval church has a Perpendicular tower and some Norman work in the nave.

B)   Of the three villages, Preston-on-Stour is the one with the greatest feeling of remoteness. Overlooking a spacious green is the medieval church, partially rebuilt in the 18th century but retaining its Perpendicular tower.

C)   The Gothic alterations and extensions to this 18th century house were an early example of the revival of this style.

D)   The church, seen across the fields before reaching the small village, was built in 1876.

24. *Warwick and Guy's Cliffe*

Route:	Warwick - River Avon - Old Milverton - Guy's Cliffe - Warwick
Start:	Warwick, in the Market Place by the Market Hall (Warwickshire Museum)
Distance:	6^1/$_2$ miles
Parking:	Warwick
Refreshments:	Pubs and cafes at Warwick, pub by Guy's Cliffe
OS Maps:	Landranger 151
	Pathfinder 976

WALK 24

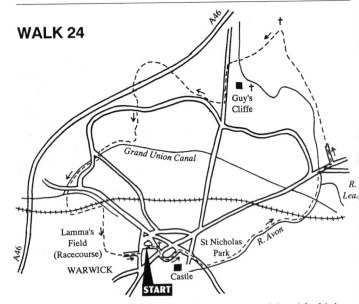

Although built up in places, especially on the return to Warwick, this is an attractive and interesting walk with a pleasant opening stretch beside the River Avon, fine views across the valley near Old Milverton, and some canal walking near the end. Historic interest is supplied by the ruined mansion of Guy's Cliffe and the many outstanding buildings of Warwick, inevitably dominated by the castle and church. Allow plenty of time for a thorough exploration of Warwick, one of England's most attractive old towns.

(A) Start by turning down New Street, turn right at a T-junction towards the church and turn right in front of it down Church Street to the main road. Cross over, continue down Castle Street and opposite the timber-framed Oken's House (now a Doll Museum), turn left along Castle Lane to Castle Hill. Turn right, pass the end of Mill Street and continue alongside St Nicholas Park to the bridge over the River Avon for the superb view of Warwick Castle.

Just before the bridge turn left, at a Centenary Way sign,

The cottages in Mill Street lie below the walls of Warwick Castle

descend steps and follow a tarmac path through the park beside the river. Cross a road by a bridge, continue along the tree-lined riverbank, going under first a railway bridge and then a canal aqueduct, pass the confluence of the Avon and the Leam and finally head up to a main road opposite the Potterton Factory. Turn right to cross the bridge over the Avon - this is the border between Warwick and Leamington - continue along the left hand road at the fork ahead and take the first turning on the left (Rock Mill Lane).

In front of a cottage bear right, at a public footpath sign Old Milverton and Saxon Mill, onto an enclosed path that passes to the right of the cottage and heads uphill. Continue first along the left edge of a children's play area, then along the edge of new housing, and the path becomes enclosed again and descends to cross a footbridge over a brook. Head uphill again and keep along the left edge of a field. Over to the left are fine views across the Avon valley. The path bears right across the field towards Manor Farm and keeps alongside a hedge on the right to pass to the left of the large farmhouse.

At a fork take the right hand path that heads across a field towards Old Milverton church. Go through a kissing gate, keep ahead to climb a stile into the churchyard, turn left by the church (B) and head down to another kissing gate. Go through and follow a path gently downhill across a field to a stile. Ahead is a fine view of Guy's Cliffe. Climb the stile, continue across the next field, climb two stiles in quick succession and cross a footbridge over the River Avon. Keep to the left of the Saxon Mill restaurant and pub to a road.

Turn left, pass the entrance to Guy's Cliffe (C) and after $^1/_4$ mile, turn right along a hedge-lined, tarmac track (Woodloes Lane). Continue along the left hand track at a fork, head gently uphill, cross a bridge over the A46 and at the next fork, keep along the left hand track again which curves left to a farm. Just before the farm buildings, turn half-left, at a waymarked post, and walk diagonally across a field to a stile in the far corner. Climb it, descend an embankment, cross carefully the busy A46 and ascend an embankment on the other side to emerge onto a green in a new housing area.

Now follows some suburban walking along tarmac paths before reaching the towpath of the Grand Union Canal. Keep ahead, cross a road, take the path ahead which passes in front of bungalows and descend to another road. Cross over, continue along the path ahead which bends right, turn left and walk along Corbison Close to a T-junction of paths. Turn right, follow the path to the left, cross a road, keep ahead along Boswell Grove and at the end of the houses, turn right across an open grassy area and climb steps onto the canal towpath (D).

Turn right, at the first bridge (no 50) climb steps onto a road, turn left over the bridge and turn right onto a path above the canal. Bear right to descend to the canal again, pass under a bridge and keep beside it to the next bridge (no 51) where you head up to a road again. Cross over, continue along Budbrooke Road and cross the Saltisford Arm of the canal by a Canal Museum. Where the road bends right, keep ahead, at a public footpath sign, along a path between high wire fences through a factory area.

Climb a stile, carefully cross a railway line, go up steps, climb another stile and ahead is Lamma's Field, now Warwick Racecourse and a golf course. Turn left along the left edge of a field, pass through a gap into the next field and in the corner turn right to continue by the left edge to a stile. Climb it, follow a path straight across the racecourse - ducking under several barriers - and on reaching a track, turn left and pass through a car park to a road (Linen Street).

Keep ahead uphill to a T-junction, turn left and after 50 yards turn right up steps to return to the Market Place.

(A)   With a wealth of fine architecture of all periods, ranging from timber-framed, medieval and Tudor structures to dignified, Classical buildings of the 17th and 18th centuries - and some later ones - a walk around Warwick is a rewarding experience. The medieval east and west gateways into the town survive, both with chapels above, and adjacent to the west tower is the impressive Lord Leycester Hospital, comprising a medieval hospital, chapel and guildhall grouped around a courtyard. Focal point of the town is the large Market Place in the middle of which is the 17th century Market Hall, now the Warwickshire Museum. Nearby is the great collegiate church of St Mary with its majestic tower, founded in the 12th century but mostly rebuilt after a fire which destroyed much of the town in 1694. In the 15th century Beauchamp Chapel are the tombs of some of the most powerful figures of late medieval and Tudor England, including several earls of Warwick and Robert Dudley, Earl of Leicester, the favourite of Elizabeth I.

Warwick Castle is often described as 'the finest medieval castle in England' and many would agree with that. It is certainly one of the most complete and best-preserved and the view of it from Castle Bridge, its walls rising sheer above the Avon, is unforgettable. Founded by the Normans, the present castle is mainly the result of a major 14th century rebuilding. Since then it has been added to and modernised several times, especially in the 17th century when the interior was remodelled. Inside is a superb collection of arms and armoury, paintings and furniture.

(B)   The church, rebuilt in 1879-80, commands a fine view over the Avon valley.

(C)   History and romance are intermingled at Guy's Cliffe. Guy was a legendary figure, who on his return from the Holy Land is reputed to have lived as a hermit in a cave by the river. The 18th century house, now ruined and not open to the public, was extended in the 19th century to give it a more picturesque appearance. Adjoining it is a 15th century church. In the woods on nearby

Blacklow Hill, Piers Gaveston, unpopular favourite of Edward II, was murdered by a group of nobles, led by the earl of Warwick, in 1312.

(D)   For details of the Grand Union Canal see Walk 8.

SOUTH WARWICKSHIRE

In two ways the Feldon that lies to the south of the Avon valley is different from the rest of Warwickshire. It is the hilliest part of the county and it is the only region where the villages and towns are built of stone. The stone is the same warm-looking limestone found in the Cotswolds, as the hills of South Warwickshire are part of the range of limestone uplands that stretches across England from Dorset to Yorkshire.

In the Middle Ages and later this was also the most prosperous part of the county and many of the villages that nestle in the valleys have fine medieval churches built from the profits of the wool trade. On the hills above a series of magnificent viewpoints are attainable from modest heights and for relatively little effort. Below one of them, the long wooded ridge of Edge Hill, the first battle of the Civil War between Charles I and Parliament was fought in 1642.

Five of the six walks in this area take you over these hills, and on one of them you climb gently to the highest point in the county, over 850 feet up on Ilmington Down. The remaining walk is in southernmost Warwickshire, an attractive circuit of four villages lying close to the Oxfordshire border.

25. Ilmington Downs

Route:	Ilmington - Foxcote House - Ilmington Downs - Ilmington
Start:	Ilmington, in front of village hall at junction of roads to Stratford and Shipston, Foxcote and Chipping Campden
Distance:	5^{1}/$_{2}$ miles
Parking:	Roadside parking in Ilmington
Refreshments:	Pubs at Ilmington
OS Maps:	Landranger 151
	Pathfinders 1020 and 1021

Although this walk climbs to the highest point in Warwickshire, 858 feet up on Ilmington Downs and close to the Gloucestershire border, there is no steep climbing but just easy and gradual ascents and descents. The route passes in front of the elegant 18th century facade of Foxcote House and on the long descent from the highest point, the Avon valley is spread out below you, with the long ridge of Edge Hill over to the right.

(A) Begin by passing to the right of the village hall, in the Chipping Campden direction, and take the first turning on the left to head up along the side of the large, sloping, triangular green. To the right are fine views over the village and church. Follow the lane to where it ends and keep ahead along a grassy, hedge- and tree-lined track.

Ignore the first public footpath sign on the right but at the second one, turn right onto a path that descends through a narrow belt of trees to a stile. Climb it, and another just ahead, turn left and head uphill along the left edge of fields, climbing several stiles, to reach a track - Pig Lane - at the top. From here there are grand views ahead over the northern Cotswolds. Cross the track, continue downhill along the left edge of a field, climb a stile in the bottom corner and turn right along the tarmac track towards Foxcote House.

The track curves right in front of the house (B), descends through a belt of woodland and continues uphill. Just after passing a house on the right, turn right through a gate, bear right and head

WALK 25

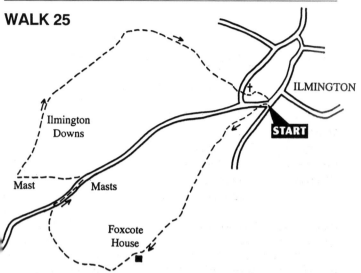

ILMINGTON

START

Ilmington
Downs

Mast   Masts

Foxcote
House

uphill across the corner of a field. Go through a waymarked gate, continue uphill along the left edge of a field and go through another gate. Follow the path through a small group of trees into the next field and continue along its right edge, curving gradually right to a lane.

Turn right and just before reaching a broad uphill track to the right that leads to some radio masts, turn sharp left through a gate and walk gently uphill along the right edge of a field to another gate. Go through, keep ahead over the brow and bear right along the right edge of a field to a crossroads of tracks in front of more radio masts. At 858 feet, this is the highest point in Warwickshire and a fine viewpoint (C).

Turn right onto a tarmac track and as you descend, superb views open up looking over the Avon valley ahead and with the prominent ridge of Edge Hill to the right. Keep along this gradually descending track for 1¹/₄ miles and about 200 yards before reaching a lane at the bottom, turn right along a stony track, at public footpath and Centenary Way signs. Where the track bends right in front of gates, keep ahead along the right edge of a field, descending to climb a

Looking over Feldon from the heights of Ilmington Downs

stile. Cross a ditch, climb another stile and continue uphill to keep alongside a hedge on the left. Turn left over a stile, turn right along an enclosed path, climb another stile and continue for another 50 yards over the brow of a hill.

Turn right over a stile, head diagonally down and up across a field to a stile, climb it and continue uphill in the same direction across the next field to another stile. Do not climb this one but turn left alongside a fence on the right, turn right over a stile and continue down an enclosed track. Look out for footpath signs which direct you to turn left through a gate, pass between sheds and follow a winding, well-waymarked path downhill, passing to the left of a thatched cottage, to emerge onto a road opposite Ilmington church.

Turn right, turn left along a tarmac path through the churchyard, passing to the right of the church, and follow the path first to the left

nd then to the right to reach a lane. Continue along it to emerge
nto a road at the start.

A)   The large and rather scattered village of Ilmington has a
ecidedly Cotswold appearance. Situated at the foot of a ridge, it
omprises a large number of delightful old cottages built of the local
arm-looking, orange-coloured limestone, greens, colourful
ardens and a medieval church. The latter is an interesting building
vith transepts, unusual for a village church. It mainly dates from
ne 12th and 13th centuries and considerable parts of the original
Jorman church survive, notably in the tower, arches of the nave
nd the chancel arch.

B)   This great house was built in the early 18th century.

C)   The panoramic views from here extend across to the Cotswolds,
nd over the Feldon to the Avon valley and the long ridge of Edge
fill.

26. Tysoe and Compton Wynyates

Route:	Tysoe - Windmill Hill - Compton Wynyates - Windmill Hill - Tysoe
Start:	Tysoe, in Main Street by the Peacock Inn
Distance:	4¹/₂ miles
Parking:	Roadside parking in Tysoe
Refreshments:	Pub at Tysoe
OS Maps:	Landranger 151
	Pathfinder 1021

*There are no apologies for what is mainly a 'there and back' walk because
he views in all directions, especially from the 600 foot high Windmill Hill,
re magnificent. Although Compton Wynyates is no longer open to the
eneral public, this grand Tudor mansion can be seen on the descent from
Windmill Hill and from the entrance, from where you retrace your steps
o the start.*

A) Begin by walking along Main Street, passing to the right of the

WALK 26

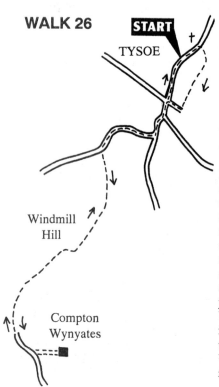

START

TYSOE

Windmill
Hill

Compton
Wynyates

Peacock Inn, and opposite the church turn right along Peacock Lane. Where the lane ends, keep ahead, at a public footpath sign, along an enclosed path which turns right to a kissing gate. Go through, turn left to another gate, go through that, turn right and walk across a field to a stile.

Climb it, keep along the left edge of a field, climb a stile in the corner and walk along the right edge of the next field, by a line of trees on the right. Climb another stile, continue along the right edge of a sports field and follow a tarmac path to a road. Turn right, at a T-junction turn left through Upper Tysoe, follow the main road (Shipston Road) to the right and after nearly ¹/₂ mile, look out for a public footpath sign on the left.

Go though a gate here, turn left along the field edge and follow it to the right to continue steadily uphill along the left edge of fields, keeping by a hedge on the left all the while, to the disused but prominent windmill on top of Windmill Hill. At a hedge corner bear left through a gap and head up to the windmill, passing to the left of it. The all round views from here are magnificent (B).

Keep ahead to climb a stile, turn right through a group of trees alongside a wall, climb another stile, turn left and steeply descend steps. Ahead are more superb views, with Compton Wynyates over to the left. Continue more gently downhill along the left edge of a

This fine windmill crowns the hill above the village of Tysoe

field, climb a stile, walk along a track and climb another stile. Keep along a broad, hedge- and tree-lined track, climb a stile onto a lane and turn left to the entrance to Compton Wynyates from where there is a fine view of the house (C).

Retrace your steps back over Windmill Hill and on the descent comes a superb view over the Vale of the Red Horse, with Tysoe church tower prominent. After following the road to the left into Tysoe, continue along Main Street to return to the start.

(A)   The strung out village of Tysoe is divided into upper, middle and lower settlements but the heart of the village, where the walk starts, is Middle Tysoe around the pub and church. It is attractively situated in the Vale of the Red Horse, so named from the figure of a horse cut into the red earth on a hill above the village. The handsome medieval church has a Norman south doorway.

(B)   The extensive views from here, looking across towards the Avon valley and over the Vale of the Red Horse below the wooded ridge of Edge Hill, are superb.

(C)   Attractively situated in parkland at the foot of low hills, Compton Wynyates is a perfect example of a Tudor manor house. It was built in the early 16th century by Sir William Compton. The house is not open to the public.

27. Edge Hill

Route: Radway - Castle Wood - Ratley - Castle Wood - Radway

Start: Radway, at road junction in village centre

Distance: 3¹/₂ miles

Parking: Roadside parking in Radway

Refreshments: Pub at Ratley, pub at Edgehill

OS Maps: Landranger 151

                  Pathfinder 1021

In the vale below the ridge of Edge Hill, rising abruptly to over 700 feet above the countryside of south Warwickshire and commanding outstanding views, the first major battle of the Civil War was fought in 1642. The walk starts at the village of Radway nestling below its northern slopes, climbs up to the wooded ridge, and then descends to the village of Ratley on its southern slopes. After regaining the ridge, it continues along it through delightful woodland, before descending via an enclosed track to return to the start.

(A) At the road junction turn towards a telephone box, just past it turn right, at a public footpath sign, along a track, go through a

WALK 27

kissing gate and walk along the right edge of a field. Climb a stile, continue uphill, by a fence on the left, and at the corner of this fence keep ahead, climbing steadily to go through a kissing gate at the edge of Castle Wood, the narrow strip of woodland that crowns the ridge of Edge Hill.

Turn left, at the fork ahead continue along the right hand path, on the waymarked Centenary Way, and ascend steps - called Jacobs Ladder - to emerge onto a road at the top of the ridge. Take the lane ahead, signposted to Ratley, and at a fork continue along the right hand lane to descend into the village (B). At the bottom of High Street turn right along a track and in front of the gate to Manor Farm, bear right to a stile.

Climb it, head uphill across a field, aiming for a waymarked telegraph pole, and then descend to climb a stile. Continue in the same direction diagonally uphill across the next field and where the field narrows, keep by a fence on the left to a stile. Climb it, turn right along the right edge of a field and continue along a track to a lane. Turn right, turn left over a stile, at a public footpath sign, and walk along an enclosed path raised above the surrounding fields. Follow the path to right and left to emerge onto a road by Edge Hill Tower, now the Castle Inn (C).

Ratley church nestles below the southern slopes of Edge Hill

Turn left and after a few yards, turn right down steps, at a public footpath sign, to re-enter Castle Wood. Keep ahead at a path junction, following Centenary Way signs again, and the path bends left and descends through the trees, passing below Edge Hill Tower. At a fork near the bottom edge of the woods, bear slightly left to continue through this beautiful woodland, keeping just below the ridge.

Just after descending a few steps you reach a T-junction; turn sharp right here and head steeply downhill along a sunken track between embankments - this part of the walk is likely to be muddy. The descent becomes less steep, and at the bottom continue along a tarmac track as far as a fingerpost where you turn right through a gate. Walk along the left edge of a field, go through another gate, continue by the left edge of the next field and in front of a tree-encircled pond, bear left to a stile in the field corner.

Climb it, walk along the right edge of a field, climb another stile and continue along an enclosed path which passes beside a row of thatched cottages and keeps along the edge of a grassy area to join a lane. Bear left into Radway and at a T-junction by the church, turn right to return to the start.

(A)   The stone cottages of Radway, some of them thatched, lie clustered around the village green and pond below Edge Hill. Despite its medieval appearance, the church is Victorian, built in 1866 on the site of an earlier one.

(B)   Tucked away in a fold of the hills below the southern slopes of Edge Hill, Ratley's steep High Street leads down to the village pub and imposing medieval church.

(C)   The battlemented Edge Hill Tower, now the Castle Inn, was built in 1746-50 by Sanderson Miller of nearby Radway Grange, architect of the Gothic Revival. It stands on the site where Charles I raised his standard before the battle of Edge Hill in October 1642 and overlooks the fields where it was fought. This was the first major encounter of the Civil War and historians are generally agreed that the result was indecisive.

28. Burton Dassett Hills

Route:	Burton Dassett Hills Country Park - Northend - Fenny Compton - Burton Dassett - Burton Dassett Hills Country Park
Start:	Burton Dassett Hills Country park, at T-junction by pay kiosk and toilet block
Distance:	4 miles
Parking:	Burton Dassett Hills Country Park
Refreshments:	Pub at Northend, pub at Fenny Compton
OS Maps:	Landranger 151
	Pathfinders 998 and 999

The open, rolling slopes of the Burton Dassett Hills rise to 630 feet and provide extensive and striking views over the surrounding countryside. The route first descends into the village of Northend and continues along the northern base of the hills to Fenny Compton. From here it heads over the flat-topped Gredenton Hill to return to the start. The two brief detours from the main route - around the village of Fenny Compton and to Burton Dassett church - are both eminently worthwhile and highly recommended.

Facing the pay kiosk, turn left along the lane and turn left off it to ascend the steps to the Beacon Tower on Windmill Hill, a magnificent viewpoint (A). Descend the steps, turn left and head steeply downhill in the direction of Northend, making for the right hand one of the two waymarked stiles in front. Climb it, keep ahead across the grassy slopes - there are several footpath posts - down to a stile, climb that and keep ahead to climb another. Walk along an enclosed track, climb a stile and keep ahead to a road in the village of Northend (B).

The pub is to the left but the route continues to the right. At a public footpath sign, turn right along a track which bears right to a kissing gate, go through and follow a path diagonally across a field heading gently uphill to go through another kissing gate. Continue across a sloping field, go through a kissing gate, bear left across the next field and go through a gate in the corner. Walk along the left

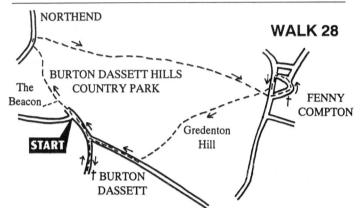

WALK 28

edge of a field, passing a barn, and in the field corner cross a footbridge over a brook. Keep straight ahead across the next field, with the spire of Fenny Compton church directly in front, pass through a hedge gap and continue across the next field. Go through a gate and head across a field to another gate in the corner.

Now comes the first of two short detours. Go through the gate, pass in front of a barn, climb a stile, walk along an enclosed path and climb another stile onto a road in Fenny Compton (C). Do a brief circuit of this attractive village by first turning left, turn right along Church Street, pass the church, follow the road round to the left, passing the end of High Street - turn right here for the pub - and at a T-junction, turn left to return to the last stile you climbed. Retrace your steps to the barn, go through the gate into the field again but turn left off the outward route and head across the field to another gate.

Go through, turn right along the field edge, follow it to the left and head uphill over the shoulder of the distinctive, flat-topped Gredenton Hill. In the top corner keep ahead to a gate, go through and shortly bear slightly left to follow a path through an attractive, steep-side valley, with the woodland of Old Burton Covert to the right. Go through another gate, bear left uphill, clipping a fence corner, and continue steeply uphill to a gate. Go through another gate, bear left uphill, clipping a fence corner, and continue steeply uphill to go through a gate onto a lane.

Turn right downhill and at a junction, turn sharp left and continue downhill for the second brief detour to Burton Dassett church (D). Retrace your steps to the junction and keep ahead, passing between Harts Hill and Magpie Hill, to return to the start.

(A)   Burton Dassett Hills Country Park covers about 100 acres of open hilltop. Some of the hollows are the remains of old quarries that were worked here during the Victorian era. The Beacon Tower was probably built in the early 16th century and along with the toposcope on the neighbouring Magpie Hill is a magnificent viewpoint. From here Warwick Castle and Coventry Cathedral can be seen, and on clear days the views extend across the Midlands to the Clee and Malvern Hills.

(B)   Northend has some attractive thatched cottages and a small 19th century church.

(C)   Cottages built of the local light brown, warm-looking, iron-bearing limestone, plus some later brick houses, line the streets of Fenny Compton. The medieval church has a 14th century tower crowned by a short spire.

(D)   It is difficult to believe that in the Middle Ages Burton Dassett was a large and flourishing village with the right to hold a market and an annual fair. The Black Death began the process of decline, but the village never recovered from the evictions carried out by Sir Edward Belknap to make way for more profitable sheep pastures, and the settlement of Southend to the south of the church became depopulated. The plain, mainly 13th century church, built into the side of the hill, is a gem. The guidebook describes it perfectly as having 'an air of antiquity and solidity which harmonises with its environment, and is recognised as one of the most beautiful and unspoilt village churches in Warwickshire'. Not even the proximity of either the country park or the M40, which runs at the base of the hills, has managed to destroy its timeless and remote atmosphere. It has a fine aisled nave, lancet windows and retains two of the original Norman doorways.

29. Brailes Hill

Route:	Shipston-on-Stour - Barcheston - River Stour - Willington - Brailes Hill - Brailes - Barcheston - Shipston-on-Stour
Start:	Shipston-on-Stour, Market Place
Distance:	10 miles
Parking:	Shipston-on-Stour
Refreshments:	Pubs and cafes at Shipston-on-Stour, pubs at Brailes
OS Maps:	Landranger 151
	Pathfinders 1021 and 1044

This is a lengthy and varied, though not strenuous walk. Initially the route keeps by the River Stour, passing though the villages of Barcheston and Willington, before climbing gently over the shoulder of Brailes Hill. On the descent into Brailes the views are dominated by the tower of its imposing church, 'the cathedral of the Feldon'. The return leg takes an undulating route across fields and by woodland back to Shipston. There are impressive and extensive views throughout, especially from the slopes of Brailes Hill.

(A) Start in the Market Place in front of Lloyds Bank and walk down High Street. Take the first turning on the left, turn right at a T-junction and follow the road, signposted to Brailes and Banbury, to the left. Cross the bridge over the River Stour and at a public footpath sign, turn right over a stile.

Walk across a field, by a line of widely spaced trees on the right, climb a stile and continue in the same direction across a series of fields and over a succession of stiles, finally climbing a stile in a field corner onto a track. Continue along the track to a lane which curves left, and where it bends left again to Barcheston church (B), turn right over a stile and head across a field, keeping close to its right edge. Descend to climb a stile, keep ahead across the field, by the winding Stour on the right, climb another stile, continue across the next field and go through a gate beside a bridge over the river.

Keep ahead along an enclosed, tarmac path into Willington (C), continue along a lane, following it around a left bend, and at a T-

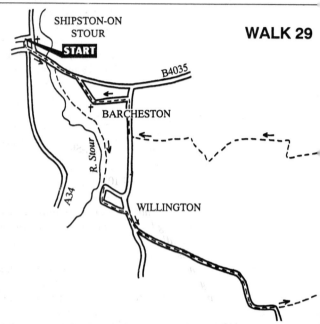

WALK 29

junction turn right. Keep along a quiet, narrow lane for the next 1¹/₂ miles and at the second right hand bend, turn left through a gate and immediately turn right through another one. Head steeply uphill over Cherington Hill, passing through a small group of trees, and go through a gate at the top onto a plateau. Continue in a straight line, across a succession of fields and through several gates, as far as a hedge corner where you go through a gate and keep along the right edge of the next field. In the field corner, turn right through a gate and after a few yards turn left through a blue-waymarked gate.

As you continue along the right edge of a field across the shoulder of Brailes Hill, there are grand views to the right, with the village of Sutton-under-Brailes in the valley below. Pass through a gap, keep along the right edge of the next field and go through a gate onto a track in front of a farm. Turn left along the track, passing to the left of a barn, and continue through a series of gates; to the right

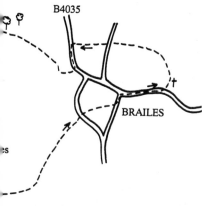

Brailes church and village come into view. Finally descend along a most attractive tree-lined path between embankments to emerge onto a lane.

Turn left, almost immediately turn right over a stile, at a public footpath sign, and keep ahead over a series of stiles in the direction of Brailes church, eventually continuing along a track and climbing a stile onto a road. Turn left to a T-junction, turn right and follow the road into Lower Brailes (D). Opposite the George Hotel, turn left along a track - Butchers Lane - beside the church and ust before reaching a farmhouse, turn left over a stile.

Keep by the left edge of a field, by a metal fence on the left, and where this fence turns left, keep ahead across the field and turn left to cross a footbridge over a brook. Climb the steps ahead, walk along a partly enclosed path to a stile, climb it, keep ahead across the next field and climb another stile. In the next field the path curves slightly left to a stile; climb it, cross a lane and climb the stile opposite. Keep along the right edge of a field, go through a gap, continue along the edge of the next field, passing to the right of a house, and climb a stile onto a lane.

Turn left through Upper Brailes and where the lane bends left, turn right along a track, pass to the right of the Primitive Methodist chapel and continue to a stile. Climb it, walk along the right edge of field, follow it to the right and head uphill to climb a stile. Turn left, continue up through an area of trees and scrub to emerge into a field of rough grass and continue across it, making for a stile in the far corner. Climb it, keep in the same direction across the next field and on the far side go through a hedge gap and steeply descend through Ashen Coppice. There are superb views from here across the wide lands of the Feldon.

At the bottom turn left and keep along the winding left edge of a field, below the wooded slopes, to reach a track. Bear right along it, go through a gate, climb gently and in front of the next gate, bear right and continue along the left edge of a field. At a waymarked tree where the field edge bears left, keep ahead across the field and descend to a waymarked post on the far side. Turn right along the field edge, at a public footpath sign turn left and walk along a broad, hedge-lined track to a gate.

Go through, keep by the right edge of the next three fields, climbing several stiles, and in the corner of the last field go through a gate beside a cattle grid onto a track. Immediately turn right along the right edge of a field, follow the field edge to the left and look out for where you turn right over a ditch at a waymarked post. Turn left along the left edge of a field and go through a hedge gap onto a lane.

Turn right, take the first turning on the left, signposted to Barcheston, and at a T-junction in front of Barcheston church, turn right onto a narrow lane. Turn left at the B4035, cross the River Stour and retrace your steps to the start.

(A) Shipston-on-Stour, capital of the Feldon, is a traditional and largely unchanged market town, with many fine Georgian houses in the streets that radiate from the Market Place. The church is mainly Victorian but has a 15th century west tower.

(B) This small, quiet village by the River Stour clusters around the sturdy 14th century tower of the medieval church.

(C) Willington is an unassuming but pleasant mixture of old and new, brick and stone, with some thatched cottages.

(D) The size of Brailes, divided into upper and lower, and the splendour of its church are clues to its former greatness. In the Middle Ages this village was an important and flourishing wool centre and market town, the third largest town in the county after Warwick and Coventry. The impressive and well-proportioned 14th century church, aptly called the 'cathedral of the Feldon', has a long nave and is dominated by its tall 15th century west tower, 120 feet high.

30. Long Compton, Whichford and Cherington

Route:	Long Compton - Whichford - Sutton-under-Brailes - Cherington - Long Compton
Start:	Long Compton, by the church
Distance:	9 miles
Parking:	Layby at north end of Long Compton
Refreshments:	Pub at Whichford
OS Maps:	Landranger 151
	Pathfinder 1044

From Long Compton the route heads up by Whichford Wood and descends into the village of Whichford. It continues across the infant River Stour to Sutton-under-Brailes, nestling below the southern slopes of Brailes Hill, and re-crosses the Stour into Cherington. The return to Long Compton takes you once more through part of Whichford Wood. All four villages are attractive, with stone-built cottages and medieval churches, and there are fine views throughout.

(A) From the church, walk southwards along the road and turn left along Vicarage Lane. Where the lane bends right, keep ahead through a gate and continue along a track below the limestone ridge on the right that overlooks Long Compton. After curving left to a fork, continue along the left hand track, heading uphill.

The track levels off and continues to the edge of Whichford Wood. Turn right alongside the wood and at a footpath post, bear left, still keeping by the wood, and soon the village of Whichford comes into view in the hollow in front. Descend along a sunken, enclosed track, continue across a sloping field and at a fork, keep ahead along the right hand path which curves left by the field edge and heads across to a stile in front of the church and large Georgian house, formerly the rectory (B).

Climb the stile, turn right through the village, keep ahead at a road junction by the war memorial and at the next junction by the Norman Knight pub, keep ahead again along a lane signposted to

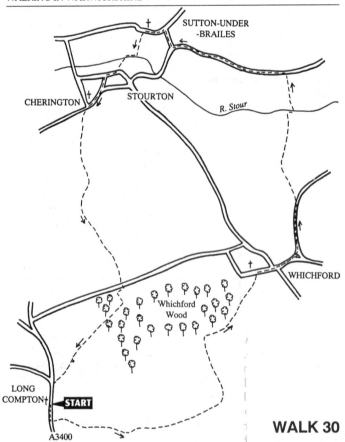

WALK 30

Ascott. At a triangular green, bear left onto a narrower lane which heads uphill and where it bears right, bear left along the gently descending track to North Leasow Farm. Keep ahead along the right hand track at a fork, go through a gate in a field corner and continue along an enclosed track, passing to the left of the former Whichford Mill. Cross a bridge over the infant River Stour and follow the track uphill to a lane.

Turn left along this quiet and narrow lane which descends to a

120

T-junction. Turn right, head up into Sutton-under-Brailes and at a T-junction by the large green, turn left and follow the lane around right and left bends (C). Just after passing the church, turn left over a stile, walk along the left edge of a field to climb another, head diagonally across the next field and descend to cross a footbridge over the River Stour again. Turn right across a field, bearing left away from the river, climb a stile, continue across the next field and climb another stile in the left hand corner. Walk along a path to a lane where the adjacent villages of Stourton and Cherington meet.

Follow the lane into Cherington (D), turn left along Featherbed Lane and continue past the war memorial, curving right to a T-junction by the church. Turn left, follow the lane to the right and take the first lane on the left which continues as a hedge-lined track. After passing through a gate, keep along the right edge of two fields, then continue along the left edge of the next field and follow the field edge to the left to go through a gap in the corner. At a footpath post, turn right along the right edge of a field, climb a stile, continue uphill across the next field and go through a gate. Keep along the right edge of a field towards a farm, pass between the house and farm buildings and follow a track to a lane. Whichford Wood lies immediately ahead.

Turn right and after 100 yards, turn left downhill along an enclosed track by the left edge of woodland. At a fork, continue for a few yards along the right hand track and then turn right, at a waymarked post, onto a track which continues gently downhill through mixed woodland. The track emerges from the trees and continues along the right edge of a field, with views of the tower of Long Compton church ahead. Keep along the left edge of the next field and then continue along a wide, hedge-lined track. After going through a gate, keep ahead across a field, go through another gate on the far side and continue to a road. Turn left to return to the start.

(A) It is easy to see how Long Compton gets its name. Its honey-coloured houses and cottages, many of them thatched, stretch for nearly 1 mile along the Stratford-upon-Avon to Oxford road. The imposing 13th century church is approached by an unusual two-storeyed, timber-framed lych gate with an upper room, thought to have been a cottage or even the priest's house. On the steep

As the name indicates, Sutton-under-Brailes is situated immediately below Brailes Hill

limestone ridge above the village, now the Warwickshire-Oxfordshire border and once part of an ancient routeway across England, stand the Rollright Stones, an impressive group of Bronze Age remains.

(B)   A 12th century doorway survives from the original Norman church built by the De Mohuns, the family of Norman knights after whom the village pub is named and who once had a castle here. The rest of the church dates mainly from the 13th and 14th centuries and is noted for the fine tombs of two 16th century rectors.

(C)   The widely spaced village sits snugly below Brailes Hill around a wide green. Its mainly 13th century church, a heavy, fortress-looking building, is unusual in that the tower, added in the 14th century, is above the south porch.

(D)   Cherington is a harmonious mixture of old and new, brick and stone, with thatched cottages and a 13th century church.

LONG DISTANCE PATHS

There are two long distance footpaths in Warwickshire.

Heart of England Way
This is approximately 100 miles long and runs from Cannock Chase, where it links up with the Staffordshire Way, southwards across the Midlands to the Cotswolds, where it links with the Cotswold and Oxfordshire Ways, finishing at Bourton-on-the-Water. Much of its course is across the West Midlands and Warwickshire, cutting through the wedge of country between Birmingham and Coventry and continuing across the Forest of Arden and Avon valley. It is perhaps surprisingly rural and explores some of the finest countryside in the Midlands.

Centenary Way
This was established in 1989 to commemorate the 100th anniversary of Warwickshire County Council. It begins at Kingsbury Water Park and weaves its way across the centre of the county to finish at Meon Hill to the south of Stratford-upon-Avon. At both ends it links with the Heart of England Way.

USEFUL ORGANISATIONS

British Waterways, Willow Grange, Church Road, Watford WD1 3QA Tel: 01923 226422

Council for the Protection of Rural England, Warwick House, 25 Buckingham Palace Road, London SW1W 0PP Tel: 0171 976 6433

Countryside Commission, John Dower House, Crescent Place, Cheltenham, Glos GL50 3RA Tel: 01242 521381

English Heritage, Fortress House, 23 Savile Row, London W1X 1AB Tel: 0171 973 3000

Heart of England Tourist Board, Woodside, Larkhill Road, Worcester WR5 2EF Tel: 01905 763436

Heart of England Way Association, 50 George Road, Water Orton, Birmingham B46 1PE

National Trust, 36 Queen Anne's Gate, London SW1H 9AS Tel: 0171 222 9251
> Regional Office: Mythe End House, Tewkesbury, Glos GL20 6EB Tel: 01684 850051

Ramblers' Association, 1/5 Wandsworth Road, London SW8 2XX Tel: 0171 582 6878

Warwickshire Wildlife Trust, Brandon Marsh Nature Centre, Brandon Lane, Coventry CV3 3GW

Youth Hostels Association, Trevelyan House, 8 St Stephen's Hill, St Albans, Herts AL1 2DY Tel: 01727 855215

Telephone numbers of local Tourist Information Centres:
Birmingham 0121 643 2514 and 0121 780 4321
Birmingham Airport 0121 767 7145/6
Coventry 01203 832303/4
Kenilworth 01926 525595/50708
Leamington Spa 01926 311470
Nuneaton 01203 384027
Rugby 01788 535348
Solihull 0121 704 6130/4
Stratford-upon-Avon 01789 293127
Warwick 01926 492212

PRINTED BY
CARNMOR PRINT & DESIGN, PRESTON PR1 4BA U.K.